MAX ERNST

max ernst

BY GASTON DIEHL

CROWN PUBLISHERS, INC. - NEW YORK

Titel page: PORTRAIT OF MAX ERNST
by Bellmer

Series published under the direction of:
MADELEINE LEDIVELEC-GLOECKNER

Translated from the French:
EILEEN B. HENNESSY

Library of Congress Cataloging in Publication Data

Diehl, Gaston.
   [Max Ernst. English]
   Max Ernst / by Gaston Diehl; [translated from the French by
   Eileen B. Hennessy].
   p. cm.
   Translation of: Max Ernst.
   Includes bibliographical references.

     1. Ernst, Max, 1891-1976 — Criticism and interpretation.
I. Title.
N6888.E7D513   1991   91-11929
759.4 — dc20   CIP

PRINTED IN ITALY — INDUSTRIE GRAFICHE CATTANEO S.P.A., BERGAMO
© 1991 BONFINI PRESS ESTABLISHMENT, VADUZ, LIECHTENSTEIN
ALL RIGHTS OF REPRODUCTION BY S.P.A.D.E.M, PARIS

SEASHELLS, 1927. Frottage and oil on paper, 16″ × 25⅛″ (4 × 64 cm)
Former collection of Alexander Iolas

A recognition too long delayed

I have always retained a vivid and precise recollection of the work of Max Ernst, with which I became acquainted on the eve of the Second World War. Later conversations with Eluard and especially with Desnos had often revived this recollection, whether it was a question of his sets for the production of « Ubu enchaîné » staged by Sylvain Itkine in 1937 at the Comédie des Champs-Elysées, his participation in the International Surrealist Exhibition in January 1938 in the Faubourg Saint-Honoré, or his collages for *Histoire Naturelle* or *Une Semaine de Bonté*, which Jeanne Bucher kindly offered to show me during my visits to her gallery, where I had also seen a small collection of his paintings and sculptures, together with bindings by Rose Adler.

From then on, certain titles and images which had literally fascinated me — *In the Stable of the Sphinx, He Who Escaped, The Court of the Dragon* — had become so fixed in my memory that many years later I rediscovered them, intact and almost obsessive. Then I was convinced: such an artist compelled recognition, with an obviousness which admitted of no discussion.

The Conjugal
Diamonds
Frottage
"Histoire Naturelle"

The Origin of the
Pendulum
Frottage
"Histoire Naturelle"

However, things did not happen as one might have expected. First came the succession of events on the international scene, of which the artist was the unfortunate victim, and which kept him away from Paris until 1953. Then, the public and sometimes the critics remained cool to him for a long time and, the artist admits, turned most of the exhibitions organized in his honor during this long period in the United States, France, and Germany into failures.

What is the reason for such an unexpected estrangement?

So many of those who were directly or indirectly involved in the conflict and suffered from its horrors are tempted, in a kind of reaction, to reject works that accuse and overwhelm them with their own responsibility. So many, too, seeking peace and quiet, merely turn away from works which seem to them disconcerting, cruel, and full of anxiety and irony. Especially in France, the wave of guilt feelings which submerged our civilization as it emerged from the agony readily attacked the Expressionists and Surrealists for having been the first to denounce the evils which that civilization ultimately discovered for itself but sought to forget as soon as possible. The triumphal flowering first of geometric abstraction and then of lyrical abstraction seemed to occur just in time to fulfill the wishes of artistic circles, to affirm a reasoned hope in which logic has its place, and to lead gradually to a collective language while allowing every individual the desired exteriorization and, as a consequence, facilitating the exaltation of the encroaching mechanization.

Despite the confusion and fundamental dogmatism blinding many minds, a turning point came in favor of Max Ernst in 1953, in Knokke Het Zoute and Cologne. However, the artist was obliged to wait for the next stages of a recognition which was so unjustly belated in comparison with many others:

1954 — His participation in the Venice Biennial won him the first prize for painting, but condemned him to a renewal of the abusive tirades of his former comrades.

1958 — The very thorough study of his work published by Patrick Waldberg fortunately filled an almost inexplicable gap, and the country in which he had been living since 1922 finally decided to confer upon him the richly deserved rights of full citizenship.

1959 — The city of Paris decided to pay him solemn tribute at the Musée National d'Art Moderne, an action which was imitated shortly thereafter by other capitals and cities — New York, London, Cologne, and Zurich.

1971 — In celebration of his eightieth birthday, a retrospective traveled to the major cities on both sides of the Atlantic.

One is obliged to admit that it was high time to make amends for past errors! However, it must be said that the reservations and rejections of this society were in part well founded, insofar as it felt by implication that it was the target, that it was being disparaged and unmasked by the work of this artist who, as we shall see, has always had the admirable ability to turn the resources of sculpture and poetry to good account in order to reexamine continually the established order and demand, with a prophetic clairvoyance, the most exigent and total freedom.

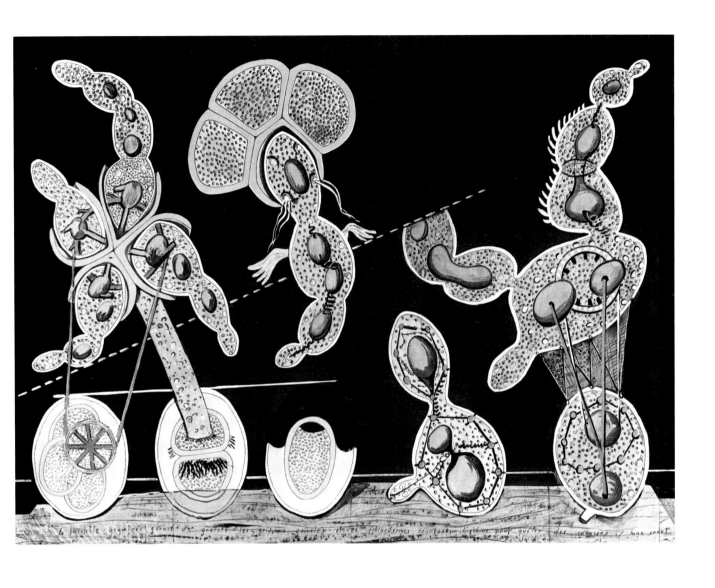

THE GRAMINEOUS BICYCLE GARNISHED WITH BELLS THE DAPPLED FIRE DAMPS AND
THE ECHINODERMS BENDING THE SPINE TO LOOK FOR CARESSES, 1920-1921
Anatomical chart altered with gouache, 29¼″ × 39¼″ (74.5 × 97 cm)
The Museum of Modern Art, New York

9

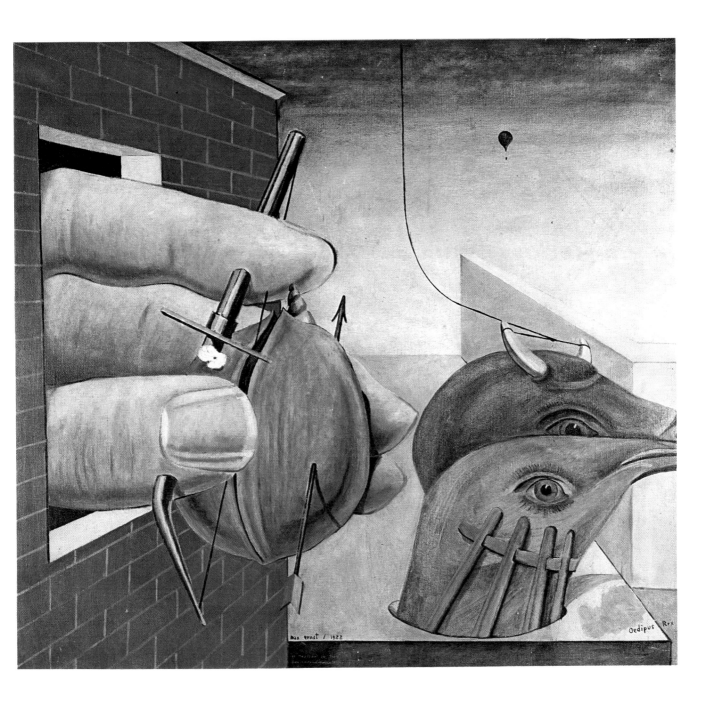

HAT IN THE HAND, HAT ON THE HEAD, ca 1913
Oil on canvas, 14½" × 11½" (30 × 25 cm)
Collection Sir Roland Penrose, London

OEDIPUS REX, 1921
Oil on canvas, 36½" × 40¼" (93 × 102 cm)
Private collection

11

THE ANGER OF THE RED MAN, 1927
Oil on canvas, 32″ × 39½″ (81 × 100 cm)
Private collection

L'emprise rhénane

O Dôme ô l'auférant que le ciel a chapé
D'azur fourré d'hermine ô grand cheval houppé
De croix dont les vertus sont celles du pentacle
Regimbe hennis renâcle
Mes durs rêves formels sauront te chevaucher
Mon destin au char d'or sera ton beau cocher

. . . .

(The Rhenish Spell

O spire! O fiery steed capped by heaven
With azure lined with ermine o majestic equine crested
With a cross whose virtues are those of the pentagram
Kick whinny snort.
My cruel strict dreams will be able to ride you
My destiny with the golden chariot will be your handsome
coachman...)

Guillaume Apollinaire
« Cologne Cathedral, » from *Rhénanes*

The first critics of Max Ernst's work, starting with André Breton in 1920, including Benjamin Péret, Georges Ribémont-Dessaignes, René Crevel, and Robert Desnos, and ending with Louis Aragon, were interested only in his current production and took no notice of his earlier work. This was the beginning of the practice of placing the birth of his work between 1918 and 1919, during the Dada period. Most of his biographers still conform to this practice, while relating several episodes from his childhood which did in fact reappear in later paintings. For years the artist himself concealed his activities before and during the war behind a « blackout » (the word is his) and dated his « awakening » from the year 1918. He undoubtedly did this in order to avoid arousing the hypersensitive nationalism which was then rampant in France, and especially in order to break all ties with his native land, which had dishonored and disowned him. Not until 1941 did he evoke the atmosphere of Cologne, to the American poet Charles Henry Ford. Later, in 1953, he gave one of his canvases the title *Old Man River (Vater Rhein)*, and in 1956 he published his « Rhein Memories. »

However, thirty-one years spent almost in a single place, in any event in a single region, inevitably « leave lasting traces, reflections of which can be found in my work, » as he himself recognized. Making use of the studies of K. F. Ertel, John Russell had already emphasized this problem in his beautiful book about the artist. More recently the research carried out by Werner Hofmann, Wieland Schmied, and especially Werner Spies, has shed greater light on the various aspects of the problem.

In my opinion it now proves indispensable, if we are to understand the complex contribution made by Max Ernst, to attribute a major role to this atmosphere in which he grew up, to the numerous manifestations of this Germanic essence with which he was able to nurture his spirit, and to that community of ideas with the major figures of German Romanticism — Novalis, Arnim, Tieck, Hofmann — which Cassou has stressed. However, this extremely important — I would almost say essential — part of his life must not

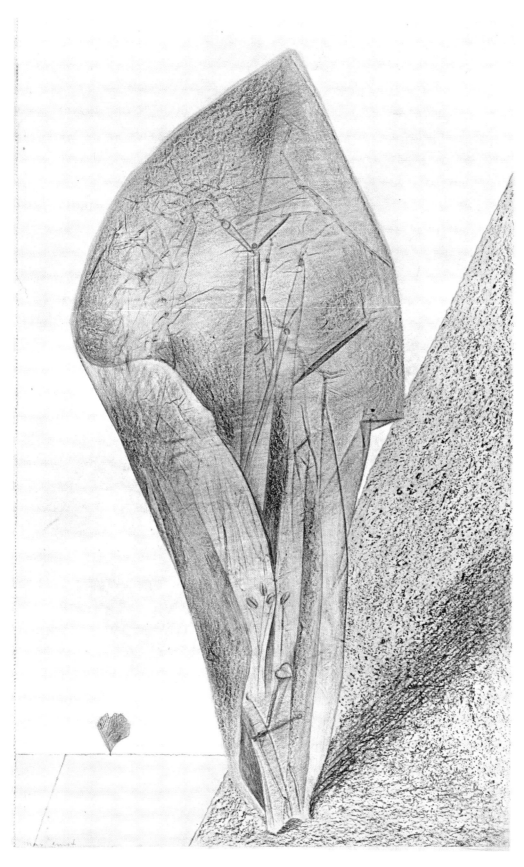

SHE KEEPS HER SECRET, 1925
Pencil, frottage and gouache
17″ × 10⅜″ (43.2 × 26.3 cm)
Collection Sir Roland Penrose, London

KATHARINA ONDULATA, 1920
Collage, wallpaper alterd with gouache and pencil
11¾″ × 9⅞″ (30 × 25 cm)
Collection Sir Roland Penrose, London

lead us to forget the inclination toward the universal which he demonstrated at a very early period. Nor should it lead us to reduce or minimize the effect of the bustle and flow of the atmosphere of Paris and the subtle amalgam of his life in France and his long sojourn in the United States which he succeeded in achieving.

To begin with, can the family atmosphere in which he was born credibly be regarded (with the frequently mentioned exception of the one psychic phenomenon, in itself quite normal, of rejection of his father) as unimportant? Conflicts with his family undoubtedly did arise. In 1920 there was an actual break, at the peak of the Dada explosion, and thereafter a feigned indifference, as is customary. However, with the passage of time nothing of this seems to survive when Max Ernst describes his parents: « Philippe Ernst, by profession a teacher of deaf-mutes, by avocation a painter, an authoritarian father, well built, a devout Catholic, always in a good mood; Luise, née Kopp … loving, possessed of a sense of humor and a supply of fairy tales. »

The family came originally from Aachen, and for professional reasons had settled in Brühl, a small town near Cologne. It was sufficiently harmonious to raise a large number of children and, despite its modest position, to permit each child to follow the inclination of his choice. Of the couple's seven children, Maria, born in 1890, died in 1896. Maximilian (familiarly called Max), born in 1891, continued his studies until the outbreak of the war. Emily, born one year after Max, became a teacher and took over her father's position. Louise, born in 1893, became a nun and died a victim of the Hitler regime. Carl (born 1894) became a doctor, Elisabeth (1900) died at an early age. The last child, Appolonia, born in 1906 and baptized Loni, married the art historian Lothar Pretzell, who organized several tributes and festivals in honor of the artist.

The fact that the rebellious young Max chafed under the paternal tutelage should not prevent us from giving more than usual consideration to the influence exerted (at least in the early days) by his father and the extremely important dual role as initiator into art and initiator into a certain mysticism toward nature which he must have played. Who else inculcated in Max the need to draw, which he revealed at the age of five, and the rudiments of an extremely detailed pictorial technique which he was still using around 1906 when he produced his first extant painting, the *Pingsdorf Landscape?* Is it not possible to imagine them visiting the museums together, admiring the Primitives and Old Masters of which Philippe Ernst made copies to order, or reading Cennini's *Treatise on Painting*, which Max was later to interpret in his own way? Is it not conceivable that, as in the case of Picasso, the Sunday-afternoon painter wished to take revenge on destiny and inspire in his heir the desire to make his inclination his full-time work? Max Ernst, for his part, states in his « Memories » that he always gave priority to what he considered the most important thing in his youth: drawing and painting.

In addition, he has not neglected to emphasize on other occasions (particularly in his conversations with Waldberg) how impressed he was, as a little child, by his walks in the forest with his father, and by the sight of a watercolor on this theme done by the latter and depicting a hermit in a clearing. For one thing, the Wagnerian myth, already quite widespread at that time, strengthened in every German heart that traditional feeling for the spellbinding, mysterious forest. Furthermore, to understand the obsessional, threatening, almost malefic aspect it would acquire in the artist's work, it suffices to contemplate for a moment the forest which still stands on the outskirts of Brühl, forming a dark wall of crowded, dense, tall pines impenetrable by the sun.

Nor did he escape — but only to resist it all the more violently later in life — that

PICTURE POEM, 1923.   Oil on canvas, 25½″ × 20½″ (65 × 52 cm).   Private collection

religious atmosphere in which he was brought up both at home and in primary and secondary school, subject to the same harsh rod which he does not appear to have valued very highly, judging by what he tells us.

By its somewhat frenzied momentum, expressionist character, blaze of color, and bloodstained sun, the *Crucifixion* in the Wallraf-Richartz Museum in Cologne, painted in 1913, is revealing in this regard. I admit that it is equally revealing of the importance of his debt to his beloved Cologne Primitives (the Master of the Barbara Legend, the Saint Severinus, Saint George, and Saint Veronica Masters, and in particular Stefan Lochner), as well as to Grünewald, Altdorfer, Baldung-Grien, Bosch, Breughel, and others by whom he was frankly inspired and whose heir and successor he would later become by virtue of his fantastic animals, enchanted forests, tortured humanity, and eloquent mineral inventions.

From Caspar David Friedrich, whom he held in special esteem, he also acquired a pantheistic feeling for landscape, which he transmuted into a propensity for magic and the occult, very natural in a region where Cornelius Agrippa and Albertus Magnus are still honored, and which he carried to the point of writing a youthful « manual » which his father hastened to destroy. His work remained profoundly impregnated by this interest, and at times he became genuinely prophetic, a fact stressed by André Breton in his « Legendary Life of Max Ernst. »

As an adolescent with an independent spirit, nervous, withdrawn, extremely sensitive to events in his family (the death of Maria, the relationship between his father and mother, the birth of Loni, the death of a pet cockatoo), all of which, according to his biographers, caused crises of depression and nightmares, he tolerated subjugation to rules and « duties » only with difficulty. In his own words, « Transient pleasures, giddiness, poems of revolt, narratives of real and imaginary travels, everything that our ethics teachers called *vanity* and our theology teachers called *the three sources of evil* (the pleasures of sight, the pleasures of the flesh, the vanities of life) had an irresistible attraction for me ... the pleasures of sight dominated. *Seeing* was my chief preoccupation. My eyes were greedy not only for the amazing world which assaulted them from without, but also for that other, mysterious, disturbing world which surged up and melted away in my dreams ... »

His instinctive rebellion was strengthened, even before the end of his secondary studies (according to him, in 1908), by his reading of Flaubert, Strindberg, and Dostoevsky with the assistance of his comrade Alfred Walter Kames, by his discovery of Max Stirner's *The Ego and His Own* and, later, Nietzsche's *The Joyful Wisdom*. These books, as Russell notes, were to become his faithfully preserved « bedside reading » which would stimulate and guide his unrepentant anarchism.

His critical spirit developed in the slightly freer atmosphere of Bonn University, where he registered with a view to pursuing a doctorate in philosophy. He soon abandoned the official, Prussianized teaching in favor of the elective courses of Johannes-Maria Verweyen, or the new esthetics taught by Wilhelm Worringer, with their broader philosophical outlook. He was particularly interested in psychiatry and in the artwork done by mental patients in a neighboring hospital, which first revealed to him the possibilities offered by the unconscious. Above all, as he says, from then on he « devoted himself passionately to painting. »

His artistic gifts asserted themselves very quickly and in striking fashion, despite his tender age. The best proof of this is to be found in the two small, carefully kept pic-

DADAVILLE, 1923-1924. Cork, partially painted and plaster, 26″ × 22″ (66 × 56 cm)
Collection Sir Roland Penrose, London

VE THE ONLY
NE LEFT
26
il on canvas
¾″ × 13″
3 × 33 cm)
ivate collection

tures which he painted in 1909, both entitled *Landscape and Sun*. The extraordinary freedom of the drawing and the saturation of the colors link them both to Van Gogh and to the German Expressionists, whom he may have had an opportunity to see during his travels in Amsterdam or Dresden. They are an astonishing prefiguration of his future themes, with the solar star irradiating the terrestrial strata, and already indicate a distinct feeling for cosmic and telluric phenomena.

Boldly, like a man who has made up his mind, Ernst threw himself into the fray. His friendship since 1910 with August Macke, who was four years his senior and was already an established painter, enabled him to immediately make contact with the Neue Künstler Vereinigung (New Association of Artists) in Munich, especially with Kandinsky, whom he admired greatly, and to participate at home in the activities of the group Das Junge Rheinland in 1911. He still harbors tender memories of this group which he joined. They were artists and writers, all of them were fascinated by Macke, and they were «united by a thirst for life, poetry, liberty, the absolute, knowledge ... Menseler, a somber and enlightened painter who died at a very early age ... Johannes Theodor Kühlemann [whose poems Ernst illustrated in 1918], several talented painters who carved out careers after a riotous youth [for example Campendonck and Nanen]; others were poets, and there were several philosophers,» such as Karl Otten, a student of Freud, with whom Ernst discussed the latest works of a master whom he revered. With them, for the first time, he was able to exhibit in 1912 in the Buchhandlung Friedrich Cohen, the bookshop which was their meeting place, and in the Galerie Feldmann in Cologne.

At the same time, starting in October 1912, he published in the Bonn newspaper *Volksmund* a series of articles on «The Berlin Impressionists,» «Art and Its Possibilities,» «The Bonn Artists,» «The Drawing Room» and others. Hofmann feels that despite their youthful enthusiasm they are already revelatory of his thinking, particularly when he decides, in connection with Kandinsky, that the artist «can feel the inner life of line and color» and give «any object whatsoever an inner resonance.»

Moreover, opportunities to broaden his horizons were constantly arising at this time, in this region destined to be a European crossroads and where major artistic exhibitions proliferated. Russell records that Cologne welcomed, one after the other: in 1911, for the first exhibition of the Gereonsklub, a group of canvases by Amiet, Derain, Van Gogh, Herbin, Hodler, Picasso, and Sérusier; in 1912 the exhibition by the Blaue Reiter group, after its inauguration in Munich; an exhibition of the Italian Futurists; and above all the «Sonderbund» which included dozens of works by Van Gogh, Cézanne, Gauguin, Munch, Picasso, and the major French and German artists. This was a genuine meeting of contemporary trends, even more significant than the famous Erste Herbstsalon in Berlin in 1913, to which Max Ernst was invited, and where he became friendly with the organizer, Herwarth Walden, the director of the art-review-*cum*-art-gallery *Der Sturm*; in 1913 the exhibition of the Rhenish Expressionists, organized by Macke, his follower Paul-Adolf Seehaus (a comrade of Ernst), and Carl Mense, a pupil of Corinth; at the beginning of 1914 the «Werkbundaustellung,» which gave Ernst the opportunity to meet and become the lifelong friend of Hans Arp.

However, in such a young man these discoveries inevitably caused a certain confusion which is reflected in the few canvases from this period still extant: *Portrait, The Storm, Crucifixion, Promenade*, all dominated by a latent expressionism in which conflicting reminiscences are mingled. Ernst tells us that he often prefers to «lose himself in his own night, permitting himself the luxury of losing his mind,» as in *Hat in the*

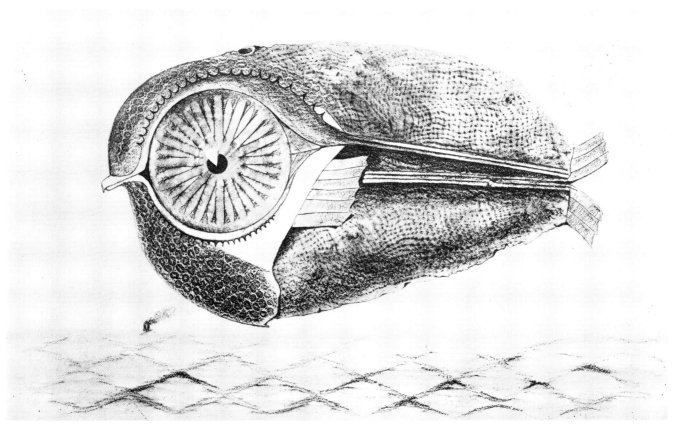

Hand, Hat on the Head, and *Immortality,* in which the transposition of reality already comes close to being the translation of a dream. His meeting with Delaunay and Apollinaire at Macke's home, his visit to Paris in the summer of 1913, and most certainly the influence of Arp, led him in 1914 into a semi-Cubist, semi-Abstract path which he followed for some time, for we find it again in 1916 in *Laon* (Wallraf-Richartz Museum, Cologne) and in the portfolio published by *Der Sturm* at this time for his joint exhibition with Georg Muche in January in the Potsdamerstrasse in Berlin. From this period, too, date his *Composition with Letter E* and *Towers.*

International events then intervened, and Ernst was separated from his comrades. He was drafted at the beginning of the war into an artillery regiment, but fortunately was then assigned to headquarters, thanks to the intervention of a lieutenant who had seen his canvases in the Galerie Flechtheim in Düsseldorf. He continued to paint and even to write whenever he could, in order, he says, to «overcome the disgust and deadly boredom inspired in me by military life and the horrors of the war.» He had the support of Walden, who was continuing his activities and deliberately remained in ignorance of

PERSON IN ANGER, 1927.   Oil on canvas, 39½″ × 32″ (100 × 81 cm).   Private collection

the conflict. While deploring the death of Macke and Marc, he reproduced poems by Apollinaire and Cendrars and drawings by Léger and Chagall, whose paintings he exhibited on two occasions.

In addition to Ernst's exhibition in 1916 and the permanent display of his works in the gallery, in August 1917 there appeared in *Der Sturm* a text by him entitled « The Evolution of Color. » While he later repudiated it, this tribute which he paid to Chagall, Kandinsky, and Delaunay seems to us extremely significant in its exaggerated lyricism and fulgurating cosmic images in which sky, movement, and nature coalesce.

« Blue recedes toward the state of total death of space, black or the cold moon, the dead moon. On the earth the sea of a vanishing blue and the desert yellow with labor are dividing. Blue and yellow are the first apparitions in color of the colored totalities of darkness and light, the measureless sphere of the firmament and the finite sphere of the earth, the first formation of the primary colors, blue and yellow. Then the blue and yellow wedding became possible: green, plant, growth multiplied. The sea and the sky continued to be the symbol of the mind, finality the symbol of man. The first prayer of the plants as marriage ». He concludes with a genuinely prophetic vision of his own destiny, speaking of « the proud biplane which will link Paris with New York by means of its astral voyage. »

He concludes with a genuinely prophetic vision of his own destiny, speaking of « the proud biplane which will link Paris with New York by means of its astral voyage. » Such symbolic harmonies of blue, yellow, and green united with the red « of life and the soul » reappear in the only work from that period that he was able to save, the small watercolor entitled *Battle of Fish,* in which the fish have strange aerodynamic shapes.

Unfortunately the worsening military tribulations left him no respite. His difficult campaigns in the Polish swamps, his assignment to Danzig and a regiment of former Death's-Head Hussars with its repugnant atmosphere, the spring 1918 offensive, then the retreat, and even his last-minute promotion to lieutenant, all served merely to feed the bitterness and rebellion that were overwhelming him and which he now wanted to express as quickly as possible.

Freshly discharged and back in Cologne (where in October 1918 he married his former schoolmate Luise Straus), he resumed his activities with a kind of passionate frenzy. In order to satisfy his long-suppressed anarchical feelings, he assumed the leadership of a local protest movement against all middle-class conformity. At the Gesellschaft der Künste, founded by the publiser Nierendorf, he had come to know one Alfred Grünwald, a young esthete, Communist sympathizer, and scion of a wealthy family (for which reason he had taken the pseudonym Baargeld). Ernst now collaborated with him in editing the magazine *Der Ventilator,* a violent social tract distributed at factory gates until the English occupation authorities banned it (after the fifth issue). With the help of Otto Freundlich, Heinrich Hoerle, and several other people, Ernst and Baargeld (despite the latter's presence, the subject of politics was avoided) set up the « Dada Central Office W/3 (West Stupidia), » which early in 1919 launched the small, short-lived magazine *Bulletin D,* the cover of which was decorated with Ernst's vignettes. He also tried to organize an exhibition, but it was forbidden, he recalls, by the English, who confiscated the catalogues and posters.

Despite the difficulty of communications, the artist must have made contact at an

THE SWAYING WOMAN, 1923
Oil on canvas, 51¼″ × 37¾″ (130 × 96 cm)
Kunstsammlung Nordrhein-Westfalen, Düsseldorf

SUNDAY GUESTS, 1924
Oil on canvas, 21¾″ × 25½″ (55 × 65 cm)
Private collection

early period with the Dada group of Zurich, since his works appeared with those of Kandinsky, Klee, Muche, and the others at *Der Sturm's* exhibition of April 1917 at the Galerie Dada in the Bahnhofstrasse, which was managed by Tristan Tzara and Hugo Ball. Later, during a trip in 1919 to Munich, which enabled him to see Klee again, he was able to learn about the latest Dada publications, whose pugnacious and destructive inclinations he shared with increasing frequency. Not by accident, his friend Arp, one of the principal figures in Zurich, joined him shortly thereafter in Cologne, arriving just in time to strengthen Ernst's daily more radical position, which tended to isolate him from his old comrades.

The illustrations he did with Hoerle for the *Der Strom* series, published with texts by Wieland Herzfelde, Otto Freundlich and others, and especially his engravings to accompany Kühlemann's poems, are still the product of his earlier formal esthetics. He had already adopted a different point of view by the time he did the album of eight lithographs he published at this time with the title *Fiat Modes*, which was viewed with a jaundiced eye by the city government, the dispenser of largesse. He was influenced, as he himself admits, by de Chirico, whose work he discovered in an issue of *Valori Plastici* which he found in Munich. He was also visibly inspired by the atmosphere of his father-in-law's hat machinery factory (where he was then working) to create series of dummies balancing in space, lost in multiple perspective and participating in scenes of a pronouncedly oneiric nature — a characteristic which clearly differentiated them from the world of de Chirico.

He continued this promenade in the bizarre, accentuating it still more in several drawings and montages composed of sometimes painted, sometimes real, elements and put together somewhat cubistically from bits of wood, letters of the alphabet, and various materials (*Dada Suburb, Fruit of a Long Experience*) which sometimes resemble an electrical installation. The machine, symbol of modern society, is for Ernst as for Picabia a kind of target for an irony which he was already dispensing liberally, in several works made of wire (*Objet Dad'art*), and in collages and drawings depicting nonfunctional clockwork trains which sometimes wore a human appearance. One of these was published as the cover for a new magazine, *Die Schammade* (Dadameter), launched early in 1920 by Ernst, Baargeld, and Arp. The three of them also organized a Dada exhibition at the Bauhaus Winter in the Schildergasse (the museum had refused to have anything to do with them); it caused a general hue and cry as well as problems with the police, who tried to close it. With this scandal the strained relations between Ernst and his father were broken off completely.

Being determined to defy the bourgeois opinion of the city, and actively supported by his wife and Baargeld, attacking family and society, Max Ernst began an open struggle against habit, tradition, and tabu in the twenty-odd objects he exhibited — reliefs, various assemblages in plastic material, engravings, sculptures (some of which, says Spies, consisted of trestles decorated with wooden molds), all adorned with suggestive and provocative titles: *I Am the State, False Archipenko, Erectio sine qua non,* and so on. The public was invited to destroy one of the objects with an axe provided for that purpose, which invitation it hastened, in its indignation, to accept. Most of the German and other writers and artists directly or indirectly associated with Dadaism were connected (at least on the poster) with the manifestation, particularly a large number of French Dadaists such as Aragon, Breton, Eluard, Ribémont-Dessaignes, and Tzara, who were now living in Paris and collaborating on the magazine *Die Schammade*. Picabia was repre-

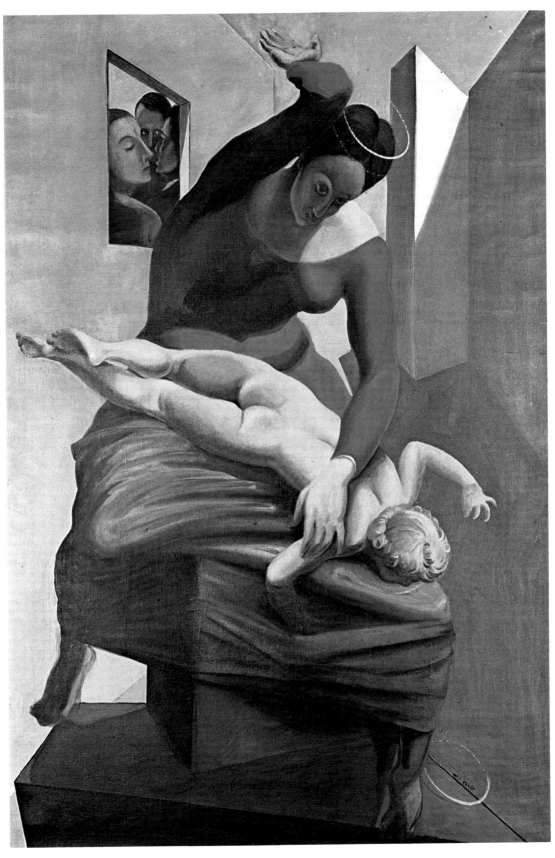

The Blessed Virgin Chastises the Infant Jesus Before Three Witnesses
A.B., P.E., and the Artist, 1926. Oil on canvas, 76¾″ × 51¼″ (195 × 130 cm)
Wallraf-Richartz Museum, Cologne

THE HUNTER, 1926.   Oil on canvas, 39½″ × 32″ (100 × 81 cm).   Private collection

LEAVES, BIRDS AND GRAPES, 1926.   Oil on canvas, 39½″ × 32″ (100 × 81 cm).   Private collection

VISION PROVOKED BY THE NOCTURNAL ASPECT OF THE PORTE SAINT-DENIS, 1927
Oil on canvas, 23½″ × 32¼″ (60 × 82 cm)
Private collection

sented by one work. Arp, who had left for Paris in January, exhibited only one relief and two drawings.

Almost simultaneously (May 1920) Picabia, with Breton's assistance, was organizing an exhibition of fifty-two watercolors, drawings, and collages by Max Ernst in Paris at the «Au Sans-Pareil» Gallery. As the second Paris Dada exhibition, coming after his own exhibition in April, it enjoyed a tremendous success. Ernst was now the leading figure both in Cologne and in Paris, as he had hoped. (He had now begun to study French.)

From this time on he occupied a privileged and unique position with regard to the other Dadaists: those of Zurich, the initiators of a libertarian, antimilitarist cortege which was no longer relevant, and who were now dispersing (several of them had gone to Paris); the Berlin Dadaists, totally committed to a relentless political struggle; in Hannover Schwitters (who had visited him), working alone on his preeminently sculptural, exemplary «Merz» montages. The Paris Dadaists were the relief force; they were regrouping around the magazine *Littérature,* founded in March 1919 by André Breton, Louis Aragon, and Philippe Soupault, and were initiating an activity which was still disorganized and inconsistent. Among Ernst's closest friends, Arp was preoccupied with research into form and poetry, Marcel Duchamp in New York was turning to erotic machines, kineticism, and ready-mades, and that incorrigible and total individualist Picabia was overflowing with imagination, projects, and travel plans.

Max Ernst had the good fortune to be able to work quietly in Cologne (the English occupation zone remained peaceful), pursuing a long-range activity and perfecting the collage, a new method of expression. While he fiercely and courageously demanded total freedom, it was not so much for the purpose of overturning the world and overthrowing the established order as it was to reexamine the work of art and its objective. Considering (he wrote) that the «role of the painter is to delimit and project what appears in himself,» his intention was to use shapes, figures, and materials in any way he chose, to ignore their customary relationships in order to arrange them in accordance with his own needs as these emerged from the subconscious or the dream. He carried on this search lucidly and persistently, however, contriving to upset and dislocate surface appearances in order to reconstruct the fragments into a strange universe which he skillfully adorned with a bantering smile and bathed in an immanent poetic grace, making use of it to mock and in a sense to ridicule all civilization. By 1919 his *assemblages,* drawings, and watercolors had become combinations of various techniques, marriages and interminglings of the most unforeseen objects — vegetable, mechanical, human, with the addition of a facetious and poetic title which lent its zest to the image and was an indispensable complement. In particular he was beginning to borrow from the collage, which he was constantly trying to improve and develop.

He was later to describe his discovery as follows:

One day in 1919 ... I was struck by the obsession exerted on my excited gaze by the pages of an illustrated catalogue which contained pictures of objects used in anthropological, microscopic, psychological, mineralogical, and paleontological demonstrations ... the very absurdity of this collection caused a sudden intensification of my visual faculties, and gave rise to a hallucinating series of conflicting images ... All that was then necessary was to paint or draw on these catalogue pages ... a landscape foreign to the objects depicted — the desert, a sky, a geological cross section, a plank ... in order to obtain a permanent, faithful image of my hallucination. »

Illustration from "Une Semaine de Bonté" or "Les Sept Éléments Capitaux," 1934

To be sure, the collage was not in itself a novelty; Mesens is correct in recalling its widespread use in popular art, ranging from the ex-voto to postcards. The Cubists had practiced it, and the Berlin Dadaists, from Haussmann to Hannah Hoch, made much use of photomontages in a satirical vein. Ernst too used the photographic montage in *The Approaching Puberty Has Not ... The Chinese Nightingale,* and *The Massacre of the Innocents,* and in the collage *Untitled* (Menil Collection), in which he exorcised both a war memory and his frequent dream of the human chisel, the flying man whom he placed on the cover of the *Bulletin D.* As Spies correctly notes, he was already making photographic enlargements of his collages so as to give them greater unity and eliminate the outline of the cutouts. He sought to enlarge his margin of action still further, and skillfully blended every possible material — drawings, reproductions, engravings (*The Hat Makes the Man, Here Everything Is Still Floating, The Little Tear Gland That Says Tic-Tac,* Museum of Modern Art) — in order to transform the basic elements, project them into a different kind of space, and leave himself open to the various appeals of the irrational.

He recalls having assembled and exhibited in Paris in May 1921, under the title « The Setting under Whisky-Sailor, » the first results obtained by this method, from *The Phallustrade* to *The Nursemaid of the Stars ... The Spring Dress of the Muse, The Shadow of a Large Dada, Ambiguous Figure, The Canalization of Frozen Gas, The Galactometric Prepuce, The Sand Worm ... Dada Degas, Dada Gauguin, Scrap-Iron Landscape,* etc.

In the preface he wrote for this exhibition, André Breton (who had been corresponding with Ernst since 1919) already clairvoyantly emphasized the fact that « We are preparing to escape from the principle of identity. » He talks about the revelations made by Max Ernst's collages in these terms:

« I remember the emotion, of a quality which has never been repudiated, which overcame Tzara, Aragon, Soupault, and myself when we discovered them at Picabia's house, where we were gathered at the very moment they arrived from Cologne. The external object had broken away from its usual ground, and its components had in a sense been liberated from the object itself, so as to maintain completely new relationships with other elements, escaping from the principle of reality but being of no consequence on the level of reality (overturning of the notion of relationship). »

Max Ernst and his wife spent the summer of 1921 at Tarrenz in the Tyrol, in the company of the Tzara and Arp families. They were all occupied with putting the finishing touches on a special number of the Dada magazine, to be called *Dada in the Open Air,* in a relaxed and friendly atmosphere which was interrupted by the arrival of Breton and his wife Simone on their honeymoon. Here Ernst made an important improvement in his method. In his collage humorously entitled *Preparation with Gelatin Glue* he made his first use of old illustrations engraved on zinc, which were easier to reproduce photographically and in which the cut edges were no longer visible.

Having missed Ernst at Tarrenz, Paul Eluard and his wife Gala visited him in October in Cologne. The poet became so enthusiastic about his collages that he selected eleven of them — related to drawings — to accompany his collection of poems *Répétitions,* which was to be published in Paris in 1922. (It was almost immediately followed by *Les Malheurs des Immortels.*) In the latter work, composed exclusively by correspondence, the prose poems are joint compositions, and the twenty-one illustrations consist of collages drawn for the most part from old engravings, admirably executed and adapted to the text, the result being a perfect artistic and poetic symbiosis.

Eluard also purchased two large, recently completed canvases, *The Elephant Celebes* and *Oedipus Rex,* which demonstrate the importance of the change in Ernst's work on the pictorial level. For the first time he had been able to closely combine certain obsessive themes of his collages — strange machinery, imaginary animals, a headless female body, objects in an unstable equilibrium, birds flying out of the sun, magical signs, etc. — and skillfully and minutiously arrange them, thus recomposing a dream world which was bizarre, coherent, and plastically valid, a world which lends itself to innumerable Freudian interpretations in which the desire to create, eroticism, masculine pride, and menacing and malign spells all play a role. Years ahead of his time, Ernst paved the way for a new, oneiric type of painting (later claimed by the Surrealists), while continuing the line of the symbolists and the great visionary artists of yore.

Simultaneously he published (1921) a poem in *Création* and a text on Arp in *Littérature,* wrote one of the introductions for Man Ray's exhibition, and participated in the « Dada Salon » in the Avenue Montaigne in Paris, just as he had earlier exhibited at the « Grand Dada Fair » in Berlin.

Everywhere, in every phase of activity (including the familial — his son Jimmy was born in 1920), he was asserting himself with authority, and at the age of thirty was showing evidence of a rare mastery. It is understandable that after a last meeting in the summer of 1922 in Tarrenz with Matthew Josephson, Malcolm Cowley, and the Arp and Tzara families, feeling himself increasingly isolated in Cologne, and encouraged by Eluard, he suddenly decided to join his friends in Paris. He was devoid of both passport and money, but on the other hand it must be stressed that he was equipped with potentialities which owed nothing to France and which he now needed only to develop and fertilize in order to attain the fullness of his gifts.

The gradual conquest of Paris, followed by
the misfortunes of an exile during the Second World War

The welcome given him by the French capital was quite different from the one he was undoubtedly anticipating. He arrived in the midst of the last bickerings and internal quarrels raging among the former Dadaists, who were in a state of disagreement after the departure of Picabia and Tzara's refusal to cooperate with the efforts of Breton, who was becoming the leader of a movement oriented more toward the problems of writing, and who now assumed the sole direction of *Littérature,* from which the plastic arts were practically banished. Ernst's situation was equally precarious on the material level. In order to survive he was forced to endure two years of hackwork in a factory which turned out souvenirs, a job which he had finally found thanks to Benjamin Péret. It was a long time before he was able to exhibit. The remarkable collages of *The Woman 100 Heads (La femme 100 têtes),* his greatest achievement in this medium, did not appear until 1929. (They were preceded, it is true, by *Histoire Naturelle,* published in 1926, the same year in which the Galerie Van Leer held an exhibition of his works.) The sets for *Romeo and Juliet* which he painted at this time in collaboration with Joan Miró finally brought him to the favorable notice of the Parisian public, and his marriage the following year to young Marie-Berthe Aurenche brought this bleak period to a happy conclusion from the personal point of view.

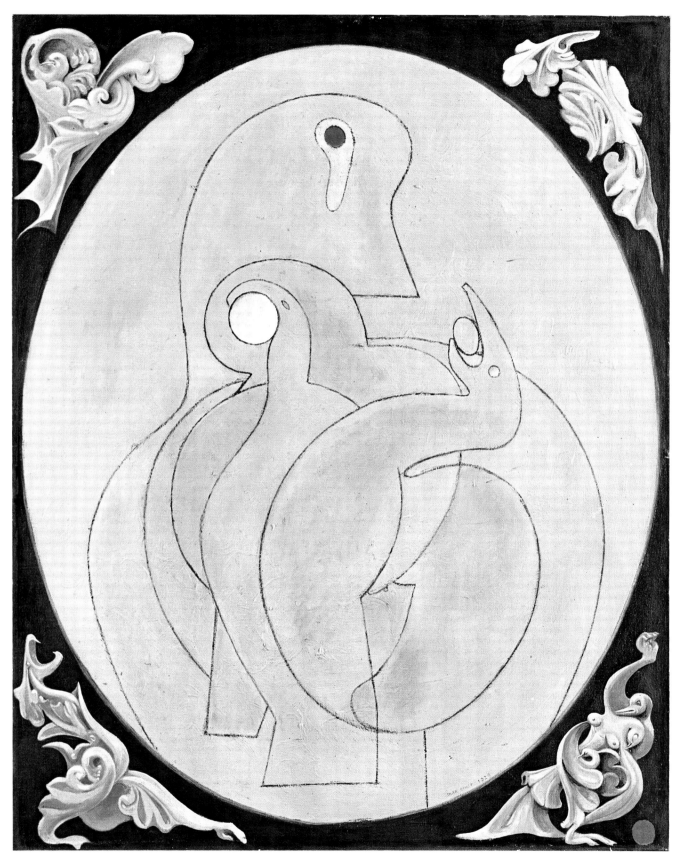

INSIDE THE SIGHT: THE EGG, 1929. Oil on canvas, 38¼″ × 31¼″ (98.5 × 79.4 cm)
De Menil Foundation, Houston, Texas

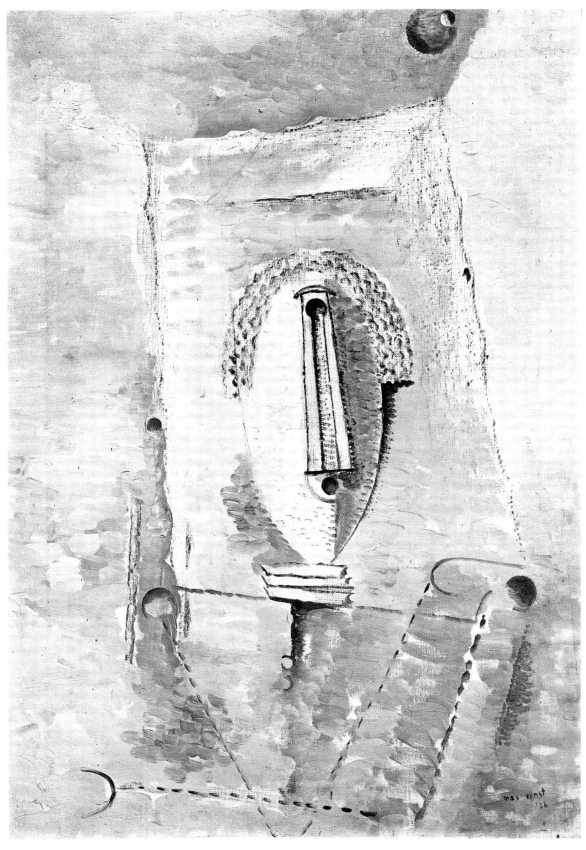

SHE REFUSES TO UNDERSTAND, 1926.   Oil on canvas, 28¼″ × 21¾″ (72 × 55 cm).   Private collection

ANTHROPOMORPHIC FIGURE, 1930. Oil on canvas, 29¾″ × 21½″ (75 × 54 cm). Yale University Art Gallery

THE HORDE, ca 1927
Oil on canvas
Private collection

AFTER US-MOTHERHOOD, 1927
Oil on canvas, 57½″ × 45¾″ (146 × 116 cm)
Kunstsammlung Nordrhein-Westfalen, Düsseldorf

La Foresta Imbalsamata, 1933
Oil on canvas, 64″ × 100¼″ (162.5 × 254 cm)
De Menil Foundation, Houston, Texas

THE ENTIRE CITY, 1936
Oil on canvas, 38″ × 57½″ (97 × 146 cm)
Private collection

Landscape with Germs of Wheat, 1936
Oil on canvas, 52¼″ × 63″ (130 × 160 cm)
Kunstsammlung Nordrhein-Westfalen, Düsseldorf

EUROPE AFTER THE RAIN, 1940-1942
Oil on canvas, 21⅜″ × 58⅛″ (54.4 × 147.5 cm)
Wadsworth Atheneum, Hartford, Connecticut

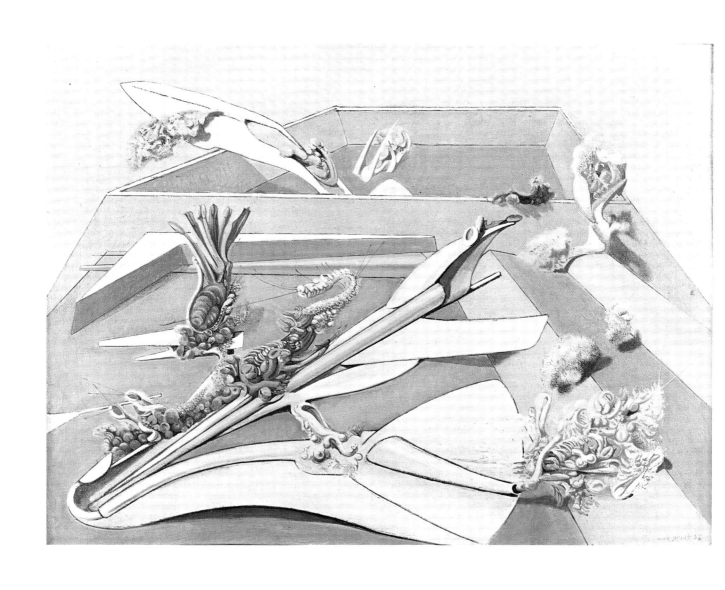

GARDEN AIRPLANE TRAP, 1935
Oil on canvas, 21¼″ × 28¾″ (54 × 73 cm)
Private collection

However, difficulties and disappointments had no direct influence on his work, which he defined and developed in masterly fashion during these years, visibly sustained by his new surroundings. During the winter of 1922-23 he participated with Eluard (who had lodged him upon his arrival) in the almost daily sessions of the so-called « sleeping period, » which brought together the future Surrealists and others: Breton, Crevel, Aragon, Péret, Soupault, Ribémont-Dessaignes, Vitrac, Rigaut, and Paulhan. During these sessions Desnos, who already had the habit of going into genuine verbal trances (related in *Littérature*), and his companions carried on collective experiments in self-hypnotism and hallucinatory seances for the purpose of inducing automatism in writing and speech. Max Ernst, who was always very fond of poetry and still fonder of magic (to judge by his 1923 canvas *At the First Limpid Word*) did not conceal his pleasure in participating in these initiatory seances, which were to exert a striking influence immediately, in several major paintings, as well as later on, in his discovery of frottage. His very large painting *The Rendezvous of the Friends* (Wallraf-Richartz Museum, Cologne), completed in December 1922, as a tribute to his hosts Gala and Paul Eluard, is a collective portrait in the Dutch manner, but in a fantastic and highly imaginative setting, of almost all the participants in the sleeping sessions plus Arp, Fraenkel, and Baargeld and several individuals of whom he was fond: Dostoevsky, de Chirico, and Raphael Sanzio — the latter not without irony, as if Ernst wished to exorcise the memory of his father, who in one of his works had been inspired by that artist's *Disputà*.

He also freed himself from several long-standing hallucinations which had remained in his memory. In 1927 he described them in detailed, almost clinical and psychoanalytical fashion in a text called « Visions of Half-Sleep, » published by *Littérature*. Sometimes they reveal a violent repression with regard to his father, as in *Woman, Old Man, and Flower* (he destroyed a first version which was too directly allusive) and in *Ubu Imperator*. Sometimes it is an episode from his childhood (*Memory of God*), sometimes a simple desire to free himself from the old restraints of his religious education (*The Immaculate Conception;* later, in the form of sacrilege and final rupture, in *The Blessed Virgin Chastises the Infant Jesus*). It would be equally easy to determine the decisive role played by personal memories, the development of the libido, and the adoption of magical signs in the particularly representative canvases *Revolution by Night, Of This Men Shall Know Nothing*, and *The Beautiful Gardener* (placed on the Nazis' black list and destroyed), also painted in 1923. These three grandiose, visionary works are genuine interpretations of dreams and obsessions, which he handles with an undeniable sureness of composition, a minutiousness and severity tempered by his instinctive irony, and in which he anticipates in masterly fashion, by his unexpected comparisons, transformations of space, endless horizons, agonizing solitudes, throbbing eroticism, and anthropomorphism, the field of activity opened up to what was to become Surrealist painting.

Some of the other experiments he was simultaneously carrying on in 1923, often with the assistance of a last admiring glance back toward de Chirico, were short-lived; they include tributes to Apollinaire, which must have been inspired by the Surrealist meetings (*Picture-Poem, Who Is the Tall Sick Man?*) and those disturbing theatrical representations of *The Last Judgment* and *Woman Bending Over*. Others, on the contrary, were pursued, and he later developed all their possibilities, as for example those collages combined with painting which he now enlarged to canvas size, such as *The Couple* (Boymans — Van Beuningen Museum, Rotterdam), with its base of bits of lace and net, *Dadaville*, in which he evokes the usual forest by using strips of cork and plaster,

Pink Birds, also of plaster, and, using the unusual montage of real and painted elements which is a summing up of his earlier experiments, his *Two Children Are Menaced by a Nightingale* (1924, Museum of Modern Art, New York), in which he raises the question of antipainting, on the subject of which the Surrealist group was soon to engage (in vain) in some soul-searching.

Today it seems paradoxical that such a number of extremely significant activities did not immediately gain public attention. To be sure, the public, poorly prepared and inadequately informed, could learn of Max Ernst's works only through his limited participation in the exhibition organized in 1925 at the Galerie Pierre, or his first exhibitions at the Galerie Van Leer in 1926 and 1927. But with the exception of Jacques Viot, who finally put him (together with Arp and Miró) under contract, Péret, who published a study in *Littérature* in 1923, and Breton's long commentary in *Les Pas Perdus* in 1924, there was an inexplicable silence and indifference on the part of the groups with whom he was constantly in contact. Despite their resolutely revolutionary attitude, for a long time these groups were actually more anxious to shelter behind the established authority of a Picasso or a Braque than to defy public opinion (always reserved, alas) by placing at the head of their movement a « German » still unappreciated despite his obvious leadership qualities. It should also be noted, in justification of this atmosphere of incomprehension then reigning in Paris, that in the third issue of the magazine *La Révolution surréaliste* Naville did not hesitate to deny all possibility of the existence of a characteristically Surrealist style of painting.

Under these difficult conditions it becomes easier to understand why in 1924 Max Ernst decided to take a trip of several months to the Far East, including Singapore and China, with Paul and Gala Eluard. But the trip brought him few satisfactions.

However, upon his return the recent publication (in October 1924) of the *Surrealist Manifesto* — to which he adhered faithfully until his break with the group in 1938 — even if it merely placed the seal of approval on the position he had adopted long before and on his unswerving early admiration for Freud, fortunately strengthened his convictions and encouraged his efforts, to the extent that he was integrated into a coherent group movement. It stimulated his pressing need for deeper study and greater freedom with regard to artistic problems. Above all it encouraged him to continue with an experiment he had already begun, and oriented him, as he explained on several occasions, toward another method « which I had been led to use under the direct influence of statements in the Manifesto concerning the mechanism of inspiration. In my personal development this method, which is based on nothing less than the *intensification of the excitability of the mental faculties* and which, in view of its technique, I should like to call *frottage*, perhaps played a greater role than *collage*, from which I truthfully believe it does not differ *fundamentally*. Starting with a childhood memory in which a panel of imitation mahogany opposite my bed had played the role of optical stimulant of a vision I had while half asleep, and finding myself, on a rainy day, in a hotel at the seashore (Pornic, August 1925), I was struck by the obsession exerted on my gaze by the panel, whose grooves had been deepened by a thousand washings. I then decided to examine the symbolism of this obsession.... I made a series of drawings from the pieces of wood by haphazardly placing sheets of paper on them, which I then undertook to rub *[frotter]* with black lead pencil. I emphasize the fact that the drawings obtained in this manner increasingly lost ... the character of the material tested [the wood] and acquired the appearance of images of an undreamed-of precision which was probably of such a nature

Collage from "Une Semaine de Bonté", 1934

as to reveal the primary cause of the obsession or to produce a semblance of that cause. Wiht a wideawake, wonder-struck curiosity, I tested all kinds of materials ... leaves and their veins, the frayed edges of sacking, the knife strokes of a modern painting, a thread unrolled from a bobbin, and so on ... I assembled the first results obtained under the title *Histoire Naturelle*. »

To justify his incursion into this field he recalled the scornful remarks of Botticelli « that by throwing a sponge soaked with various colors against a wall you would make a stain on it in which there would be a beatiful landscape, » and the wise admonitions of Leonardo da Vinci in his *Treatise on Painting* that « You stopped to look at the stains on the walls, the ashes in the hearth, the clouds, the brooks: and if you look at them closely, you will discover most admirable contrivances therein. »

In a statement of position made in 1936, Max Ernst could justly claim that the experiments he carried out alone with a lucid and rigorous spirit played a determining role. He enumerates them one by one: the collage, which made possible « the masterly eruption of the irrational into every aspect of art, poetry, science, fashion, the private life of individuals, the public life of nations, » and even « Surrealist films; that other conquest of the collage: Surrealist painting, at least as regards one of its many aspects, in this case the one which I alone developed, between 1921 and 1924; the systematic fusion of the thoughts of two or more authors in a single work » which he practiced with Baargeld, Arp (*Fotagaga*), Eluard (*Les Malheurs des Immortels*), and in an unfinished book, *Et suivant votre cas* (1923). Lastly, « I advanced alone cautiously in the still unexplored forests of frottage. » This image is completely justified. His new method did in truth offer him the opportunity to gradually rediscover the haunting memories and visions repressed within him during his childhood pitted against the sylvan shadows, and to finally liberate himself from them. He was equally happy at having succeeded in achieving a genuine automatism in art on the level of that of his poet friends, and, in his words, « at reducing the active role of the party who until now was called the *author* of the work to its lowest point. » Henceforth the latter « attends as a spectator, indifferent or enthusiastic, at the birth of the work, and observes the phases of its development. »

While he readily admits that other methods similar to frottage — *grattage* (scraping), *éclaboussage* (spattering), *coulage* (pouring), *fumage* (smoking), decalcomania, and so on — were later utilized by certain artists and by himself in his painting, he refused to condone the attitude (« a disturbing resignation ») of those who « are satisfied to produce splotches while foregoing their privilege of playing freely with them, thus abandoning to the spectator the role of interpreting them. » For his part, he did not limit himself « to looking attentively at the splotches obtained and completing the drawing by giving free rein to the play of associations »; he claims to achieve a « forcing of inspiration » and to thoroughly prospect this « field of vision limited solely by the *capacity of the mental faculties to be excited.* » With a deft pencil he unveils and demarcates with precision an entire world which has surged up directly from the mists of the subconscious, but over which he exerts an effective control — a clashing phantasmagoria always on the middle ground between animal, vegetable, mineral, and the visceral, a swarming world of phantoms and chimeras trapped in the memory-forests of his childhood, in which an unutterable anguish is lurking.

Through the efforts of the Galerie Jeanne Bucher, a selection of thirty-four drawings with humorous titles invented by their creator, and preceded by a text rich in poetic imaginativeness written by Arp, was reproduced by phototype and published in 1926,

SEA, SUN, EARTHQUAKE, 1931. Oil and wallpaper on canvas, 28¼″ × 23½″ (72 × 60 cm). Private collection

EUCLID, 1945. Oil on canvas, 25½″ × 22½″ (65 × 57.5 cm). De Menil Foundation, Houston, Texas

L' "Heure Bleue," 1946-1947.   Oil on canvas, 39½″ × 35¾″ (100 × 91 cm).   Private collection

LE GRAND ALBERT (ALBERTUS MAGNUS), 1957. Oil on canvas, 60″ × 42″ (152.4 × 106.7 cm)
De Menil Foundation, Houston, Texas

with the significant title of *Histoire Naturelle*. The original plates were exhibited the following year in Brussels. The public, and especially literary and artistic circles, were attracted by the novelty of the method, which left to each individual a large margin for his dreams, beyond the hallucinatory and detailed evocations of wild horses, ghostly flowers, enigmatic silhouettes, an astral universe, geological cross sections, and especially animals from another era.

Max Ernst was the first to make use of this throng of images and accidental encounters to effect a complete renewal of his themes. In his paintings an increasing divergence, almost a divorce, arises between the peaceful figures of people and birds, the still lifes born of unexpected Cubist and purist reminiscences and supplemented by *grattages*, plays of material (*Two Sisters, She Refuses to Understand, Leaves, Birds and Grapes*), and the premonitory dreams and alarming forebodings which are already visible in *The Joy of Living* and *The Beautiful Season*, and soon explode in gesticulating embraces (*One Night of Love*) and intermingled and jagged forms preyed on by a tormented violence (*The Hunter*). The dramatic ascent culminates in 1927 with the visionary unfolding of *The Horde*, with its distressing swarm of larvae. Its very titles reflect the oppressive atmosphere: *Young Men Trampling on Their Mother, Two Girls and a Monkey Armed with Rods, Shouting Women Crossing a River, Vision Provoked by the Words «the Immovable Father,»* and so on, complemented by the customary sinister forest scenes (*Gray Forest, Vision Provoked by the Nocturnal Aspect of the Porte Saint-Denis*), in which the birds are captives (*Bird in the Heart of the Forest*).

Meanwhile, he made a conspicuous entrée on the Parisian art scene, escorted by his poet friends, whose comments on his canvases rivaled one another in daring associations: Eluard, Desnos, Péret on the occasion of his exhibition at the Galerie Van Leer in March 1926, which assembled thirty paintings and eighteen drawings and photographs. Crevel declared that «the curtain of sleep fallen on the boredom of the Old World rises for surprises of stars and sand», in connection with his exhibition at the Galerie Georges Bernheim in December 1928 of fifty paintings assembled around the theme «His birds, his new flowers, his flying forests, his curses, his satans», in accordance with the characteristic titles of the works.

There was no doubt that he was now in a fair way to win the battle, secure in the knowledge that he was being backed by enthusiasts (the Vicomte de Noailles was publicly proclaiming his support, and there was the ever-vigilant friendship of Roland Penrose) and by several Paris, Brussels, and even German and American art galleries (Flechtheim exhibited him in 1929 in Berlin and Düsseldorf, and Julien Levy in 1931 in New York). Above all, his successful romantic adventures seemed to brighten his work, adorned with a smile of complicity, with a new dawn, giving rise to the series of flower-carpeted deserts and blossoming crystallizations (*Flower Spines*) and even more to a joyous soaring movement, at first swarming and chaotic (*Blue and Pink Doves*) or whirling (*After Us-Motherhood*), which quickly becomes lighter and lofty in the numerous versions of the *Monument to the Birds*, and ends in 1929, with an authoritative cry of victory, in the symbolic *The Interior of Sight and Brick from La Cadière d'Azur*, in which he combines in his elliptical graphism the satisfaction of the conqueror, the sign of the heart, with the proud assurance of the omnipresent creator, unchallenged master of his kingdom.

Shortly thereafter he even became identified for several years with his own creature, the fabulous «Loplop», half-winged and half-human, who domineers with a

▷

Woman of Tours, 1960
Cast in iron

58

sarcastic air over the destiny of anybody and everybody, in a series of collage paintings entitled *Loplop Introduces.* Moreover, by a phenomenon of balancing and instinctive opposition continually present in Ernst, in *La Femme 100 têtes* he had already pushed to the point of giddiness a veritable delirium, organized with enjoyment and subtlety. Ernst completed this monumental masterpiece of collage, published in 1929, in two weeks in the Ardèche, with an astonishing virtuosity, using popular turn-of-the-century engravings taken from the *Magasin Pittoresque, La Nature,* and similar periodicals. In it he succeeded in juggling every probability and every relationship, in transforming proportions, distances, feelings of space and equilibrium. No reader can resist this strange fascination, and everyone finds himself plunged into the midst of the most extravagant dreams, which by a kind of magical quality have become almost plausible and coherent, so great is their power of persuasion which overturns and annihilates all reference to a reality recalled only (and then humorously) by their titles. Thanks to this success, another, somewhat less consistent group of collages, *Dream of a Little Girl Who Wanted to Enter Carmel,* appeared the following year, also published by the Editions du Carrefour.

Why, when things were going along so smoothly, did Max Ernst encounter new difficulties and feel the need to change course? Sensitive to the weight of internal and external events and to the clouds piling up on the horizon, like a barometer he registered the variations of the moment and the premonitory signs of the coming crises.

Although he participated in the Surrealist exhibition (for which he collaborated with Tzara on an introduction) at the Galerie Pierre Colle in 1933, organized a very small exhibition in Zurich in 1934, and was well represented at the international exhibitions of Surrealism in London in 1936, New York in 1936–1937, and Paris in 1938, he often felt at odds with the group and finally broke off relations with them in 1938 because of their treatment of Paul Eluard, to whom he was very close. Similarly, his contacts with the Surrealist magazines — first with *Le Surréalisme au Service de la Révolution,* 1930–33, later with *Minotaure* — were sporadic, and he received much better support from the *Cahiers d'Art,* which exhibited his work on two occasions and devoted a special issue to him in 1937.

His series of romantic affairs with Meret Oppenheim in 1933, Leonor Fini in 1935, and Leonora Carrington in 1937–38 occasionally left traces of exaltation or bitterness in his work. However, his major preoccupations very soon turned to the rise of the Hitler menace, the tragic consequences of which he foresaw and of which he was one of the first victims (in 1933 his name was placed on the list of those outlawed by the regime). Once again he was developing symbolic and premonitory themes, repeating them insistently, accenting them each time with increasing drama, as if he instinctively wished to alert public opinion and sound an unforgettable warning.

Proceeding by vivid allusions, like repeated nightmares from which he was liberating himself with a rending irony, he foretold the death lurking and the destructions promised. In 1933 he denounced the ravages of the cataclysm in the pitiful shriveled map of *Europe After the Rain* and the cities buried under the ruins (*The Entire City*). In 1934 he evoked the menace sweeping down from the sky in the very colorful, detailed series of the *Garden Airplane-Trap,* and the unforeseeable acts of human violence in his vast collage *Une Semaine de Bonté.* In 1937 he called to mind the cunning appetites which unfold everywhere in nature (*The Nymph Echo, The Joy of Living*). The ballet was completed in 1937, sometimes with a furious saraband of genuinely demonic figures mockingly christened *The Triumph of Love* and *The Angel of Hearth and Home.* As

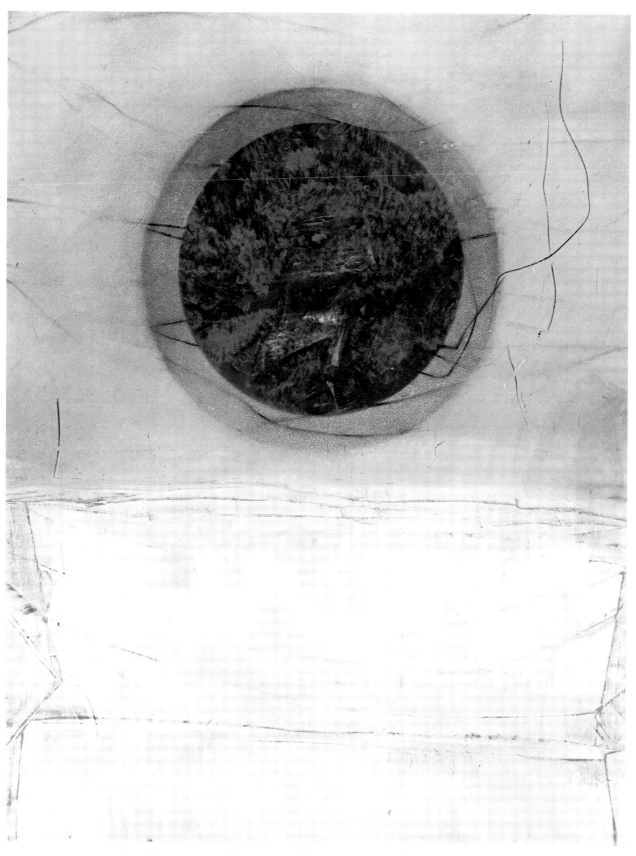

THE MARRIAGE OF HEAVEN AND EARTH, 1962.   Oil on canvas, 23″ × 35″ (116.2 × 88.9 cm)
De Menil Foundation, Houston, Texas

WHEN SIRENS AWAKE REASON GOES TO SLEEP, 1960
Oil on canvas, 25½″ × 21¼″ (65 × 54 cm)
Private collection

PAINTING FOR YOUNG PEOPLE, 1943
Oil on canvas, 24‴ × 30‴ (61 × 76.2 cm)
De Menil Foundation, Houston, Texas

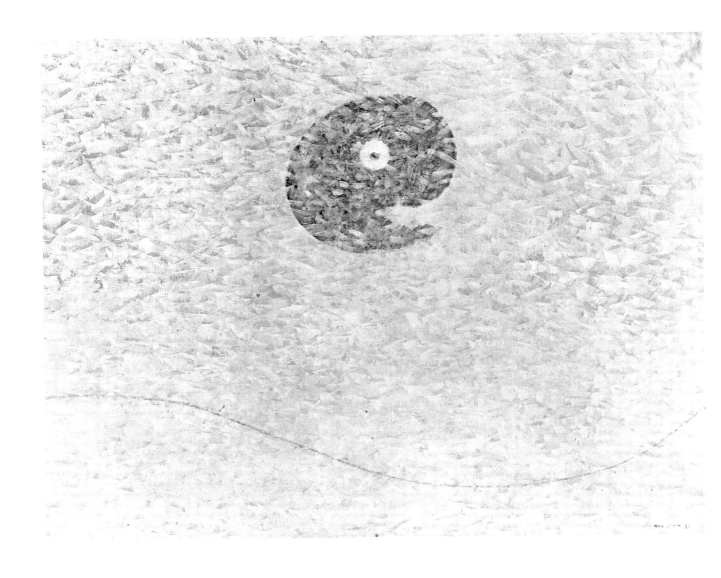

THE CRY OF THE GULL (MÖWENSCHREI), 1953
Oil on canvas
38″ × 61½″ (97 × 130.5 cm)
De Menil Foundation, Houston, Texas

33 LITTLE GIRLS SET OUT TO HUNT
THE WHITE BUTTERFLIES, 1958
Oil on canvas, 54¾″ × 42½″ (139 × 108 cm)
Beyeler Gallery, Basel

Monument t
the Bir
1928-192
Oil on canv
57¼″ × 37¾
(145.5 × 96.5 cr
Private collectio

"Sérénité", 196
Oil on canva
36″ × 28½
(92 × 73 cn
De Men
Foundatio
Houston, Texa

THE EARTH WITH A LIE ON ITS LIPS, 1960-1962.   Painting on wood, 13″ × 9⅓″ (33 × 24.5 cm)
De Menil Foundation, Houston, Texas

usual, these works are in striking contrast to the handful of earlier themes which are more peaceful but no less burdened with anxiety (*Blind Swimmer, Landscape with Germ of Wheat*).

Being completely disgusted with the disagreements within the Surrealist group and the rapid degeneration of the international situation, in 1938 Max Ernst retired with Leonora Carrington to Saint-Martin-d'Ardèche, to a deserted farm which he partly rebuilt with his own hands and decorated with wall reliefs executed in concrete. His summer vacation at Maloja in Switzerland in 1934 with Alberto Giacometti had awakened in him the desire to return to sculpture, as is evidenced at this period by *Lady Bird* and the very humorous creature *Gay*. In contrast, by their very titles and their image of a festering, Protean nature with its menacing excrescences, the few canvases painted in 1939 in the Ardèche — *A Moment of Calm, The Fascinating Cypress* — reflect his state of mind at that time: resigned and expectant in the face of the solemn events brewing. Their brutal outbreak did not surprise him, and from then until July 14, 1941, the date of his arrival in New York, he philosophically endured all the consequences of the war.

However, far from sparing him during the two intervening years, destiny had reserved the worst blows for him. It drove Leonora into insanity and led Ernst himself on various occasions to the brink of catastrophe in a ferocious game of hide-and-seek, since he was both condemned by his native land and hunted down by the French as an alleged German citizen. We shall not go into detail concerning his adventures (they have been related by Waldberg), but shall merely recall that he was arrested at the outbreak of the hostilities and stayed in several internment camps (Largentière, Les Milles near Aix, Loriol, and Saint Nicolas near Nîmes), from all of which he succeded in getting out, escaping, or being liberated, returning each time to his work at Saint-Martin-d'Ardèche. In December of 1940 he fled to Marseille. Here he became acquainted with Peggy Guggenheim, who purchased some of his works. His fellow refugees quartered at the Château Air-Bel included almost all of the Surrealists, with whom he was now reconciled. In May 1941 he and his cargo of canvases crossed the Spanish frontier at Canfranc without difficulty, but he was forced to remain in Lisbon for two months before finally reaching the United States, where his son Jimmy had paved the way for his arrival.

The fact that in the midst of continual adventures of this kind Max Ernst was able, as if by miracle, to paint several particularly important pictures is one more demonstration of the depth of his commitment to painting, which in defiance of external circumstances continued to be his major preoccupation and, as it were, his only valid reason for living. At the height of the storm, with his inspired gift of prophecy, he already glimpsed in his decalcomanias *Maiden's Dream About a Lake* and *The Stolen Mirror*, the calm of the return to harbor, the longed-for union of the vegetable, mineral, and human kingdoms, the romantic escape toward the Aztec city arisen from the waters, the warm promise of feminine embraces and girl-flowers.

The time of fulfillment finally arrives
or,
From New York to Paris,
From Sedona to Huismes and Seillans

Despite his expectations, his mishaps were by no means at an end. Upon disembarking in New York he was again interned as a German national — but this time for

THE BOTTLE
"HERE THE ACTION IS SIMPLE"
Oil on plaster (wall decoration)
15¼″ × 7½″ (39 × 19 cm)
Private collection

▷

THE BIRDS
Ink and colored pencils
Original drawing used for the etching
for "Les Chiens ont soif"
by Max Ernst and Prévert

71

only three days — on Ellis Island. The welcome given him by the American circles among whom he traveled in various states was very reserved, and his art was not highly appreciated, except among a small group of young painters and poets. Nevertheless, in 1941 and 1942 he serenely continued to dream his earlier dream of a return, increasingly tinted with black humor, to a proliferating, primitive, wild nature. The result was his series of majestic decalcomanias, *The Harmonious Breakfast* (done in Santa Monica), *Napoleon in the Wilderness, Europe After the Rain II*, and *Totem and Taboo*, and completed in 1944–1945 with the sarcastic rictus of *Everyone Here Speaks Latin* and *The Temptation of Saint Anthony*.

His marriage to Peggy Guggenheim very soon failed, and after several months he abandoned the luxurious private home on Beekman Place and returned to the difficult life to which he was accustomed. His exhibitions in New York, Chicago, and New Orleans were also, he confesses, «a complete flop,» despite the publication in April 1942 of a special issue of Charles Henry Ford's magazine *View*, in which Henry Miller, Parker Tyrel, Amédée Ozenfant, and André Breton participated. At the end of this same year his meeting with Dorothea Tanning brought him the consolation he so greatly needed, but in order to work in peace he was then obliged to take refuge with her for several months in the solitude of the Arizona desert.

From there, while casting an almost tender glance back to the past and drawing up a detailed inventory of his experience in his *Vox Angelica*, a vast synthesis of his work painted in sections, he launched with bold excitement into a complete renewal of his method of expression and themes. As early as 1942, in his need to anticipate developments, he broke new paths which he left to others to explore. In *Day and Night*, and even more in *Surrealism and Painting*, he proudly gave the star role to the subconscious and the creative instinct; in *The Bewildered Planet* and *Abstract Art, Concrete Art* (later to be called *Young Man Intrigued by the Flight of a Non-Euclidean Fly*) in particular, he favored the fortuitous by projecting the painting through a box with holes in it which he balanced over the canvas. (This method was soon taken up by the New York School under the name « dripping. »)

During these years he showed a preference for imperious, haughty masks — *Euclid, The Cocktail Drinker, Natural Geometry*. This series culminated in 1947 with *Chemical Nuptials*, which had an undeniable spiritual kinship with the Primitives. Did this return to the sources dear to his exile's heart, as evidenced by *Rhenish Night* (1944), help him to forget the increased difficulties and the repeated failures of his New York exhibitions despite the efforts of his friends? Did he hope in this way to transpose and sublimate the more tranquil moments he enjoyed in the company of Dorothea at Sedona, where he built a house and in 1947 began to do mural and monumental sculptures, such as *Capricorn?*

In any event, the plainly displayed optimism of his rediscovery of humanity and especially nature shone forth after 1946 in the minuscule paintings with poetic accompaniment which he called *Seven Microbes Seen Through a Temperament*. Upon contact with vast spaces this optimism became an epic inspiration capable of arousing in him the rebirth of the cosmic drive of yore in singing, powerful canvases — *Two Foolish Virgins, Bird, Sun and Sea, Birds and Oceans*, and especially in the series *Colorado, Raft of Medusa* and *Pink Bird*, both painted later in Paris.

This warm tide never again deserted him, not even when, after some hesitation in the face of the difficult conditions awaiting him, he decided in 1953 to return to the

THE FÊTE AT SEILLANS, 1962
Oil on canvas, 55¼″ × 79″ (140 × 200 cm)
Former collection of the artist

"Portrait d'Ancêtre", 1965.   Oil and collage on wood, 45¾″ × 38¾″ (116 × 89 cm)
Former collection of the artist

SAINT SULPICE, 1965.   Collage on plywood, 45¾″ × 38¾″ (116 × 89 cm)
De Menil Foundation, Houston, Texas

"Le Caveau des
Innocents," 1967
Collage on wood
32¼″ × 19¼″ (83 × 49 cm)
Former collection of
Alexander Iolas

▷

"À travers les Âges,"
1970
Collage, 12½″ × 9½″
(32.2 × 24.2 cm)
Former collection of
Alexander Iolas

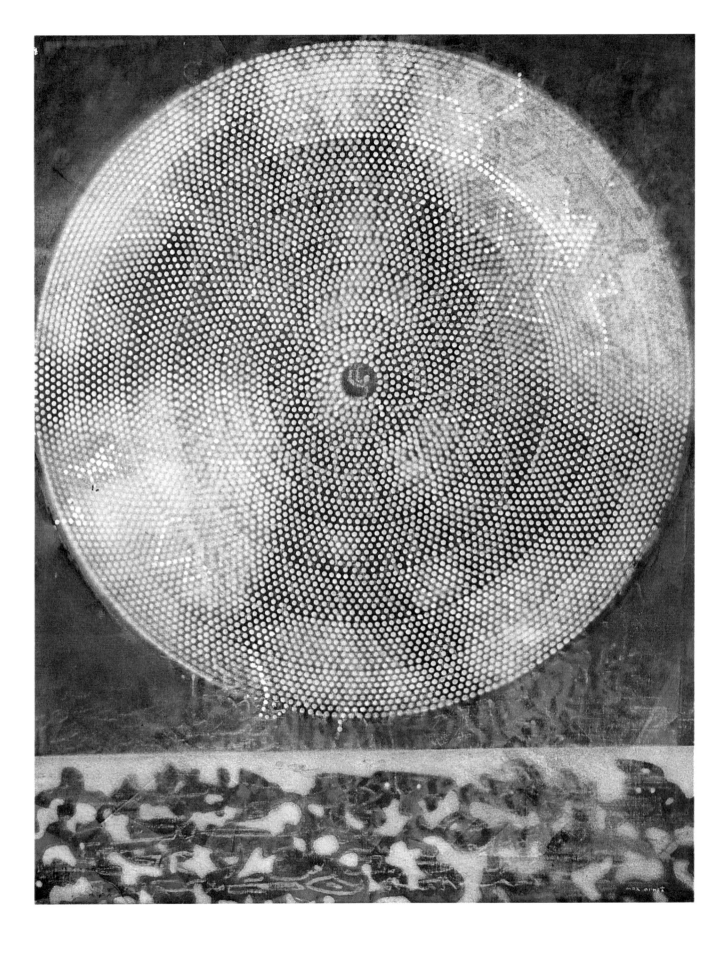

BIRTH OF A GALAXY, 1969
Painting on canvas, 36″ × 28½″ (92 × 73 cm)
Former collection of Alexander Iolas

TANGLED LIGHTNING, 1969
Painting on canvas, 31⅓″ × 26½″ (81 × 65 cm)
Former collection of Alexander Iolas

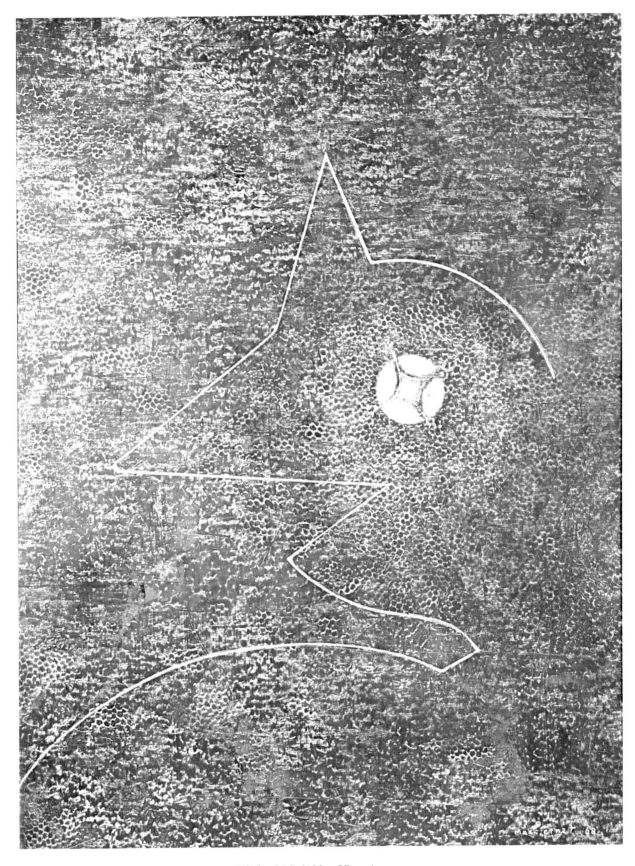

October, 1968. Painting on canvas, 51¼″ × 38″ (130 × 97 cm)
Former collection of Alexander Iolas

French capital, where he had made a short but disappointing visit when Péret's book *La Brébis galante*, with Ernst's illustrations, was published there in 1949.

Everyone who had until now made an effort to help him had encountered little more than disappointments: in the United States Robert Motherwell, William Copley, and Mrs. Jean de Menil; in Germany Loni and Lothar Pretzell. In Paris his friends had not neglected to recall his presence, at the Salon d'Automne in 1944 and the International Exhibition of Surrealism in 1947, and to pay tribute to him at the Galerie Denise René in 1945, and particularly in 1950 at the Galeries La Hune and René Drouin, with a remarkable introduction by Joë Bousquet.

But after 1953, thanks to retrospectives in Knokke Het Zoute and the Galerie Der Spiegel in Cologne, and especially after 1954, when he unexpectedly won the first prize at the Venice Biennial, destiny proved frankly favorable to him. Upon his arrival in Paris he was resolute and full of confidence, despite his quite difficult situation: a lodging under the gables of a building on the Quai Saint-Michel, a studio, loaned by Copley, in the Impasse Ronsin. But as usual he saw ahead to the outcome, and now, benefiting from Dorothea's stimulating presence, in *Old Man River* (*Vater Rhein*) he tentatively proclaimed a message of hope and reconciliation. Nature blends with phantasms, and in *The Song of the Frog* and *The Cry of the Gull* (1953) sets about absorbing them into a joyful shimmer of blue and orange variegated patterns which tend to blossom into luminous tremors (*Mother and Children in a Sunlit Wood*, *33 Little Girls Set Out to Hunt the White Butterflies*, both painted in 1957, and *A Tissue of Lies*, 1959), or harmonious seductions with a pure plastic lyricism, as in *The Marriage of Heaven and Earth* (1962), *The Fête at Seillans* (1964), and *A Nest of Swallows* (1966).

Still prostrate and imprisoned in the sarcastic *In Praise of Freedom* — an unequivocal condemnation of all places of detention and the camps of death — the familiar bird of yesteryear reappears, more mischievous than ever, in *Messalina as a Child* and *Fable Picture*, and at last frolics gaily in the witty montage *Woman, House, Sparrow* and in the smiling canvas so deservedly entitled *The Drum Major of the Heavenly Army*. Even the masks lose their stern appearance and again become an amusing cortege and a pleasant disguise (*Sunday Afternoon on the Champs-Elysées*, *Diptych for a Pirate School*, *Blacksmith of Dreams*, *The Earth Is a Chaffinch*). Did not Ernst set an example, as Waldberg recalls, by organizing costume parties and fireworks displays at his farm at Huismes near Chinon, where he spent a part of every year between 1955 and 1968, the date of his retirement to Seillans?

His zest burns and spreads with renewed ardor throughout his work. While his *frottages* (*Glimmer Chips*), drawings (*Poets' Laughter*), and collages with titles (*Commonplaces* and *Brainings*), to which he frequently returns of late, remain faithful to a humor which is occasionally abrasive, and his many large sculptures, which he creates for relaxation, are still somewhat ambiguous (*Teachers for a Butchers' School*), elsewhere serenity triumphs, and a 1972 canvas already bears this title. He gives free rein to his quick imagination in a series of montages-collages, disarming in their simplicity but rich in poetic invention and subtle in style, and bearing comments of unequaled whimsy. They were exhibited in 1965 at the Galerie Iolas under the title *The Anthropology Museum, followed by Fishing at Sunrise. Portrait of an Ancestor, Saint Sulpice, Laity, Soliloquy, Sanctuary*, and above all *The Froggies' World*, a direct outgrowth of the graphic work and secret language composed for *Maximiliana* — each and every work radiates freshness and delicate irony. The works in the next series, also exhibited at the Galerie

Twin Souls
1961
Cast in bronze and plaster

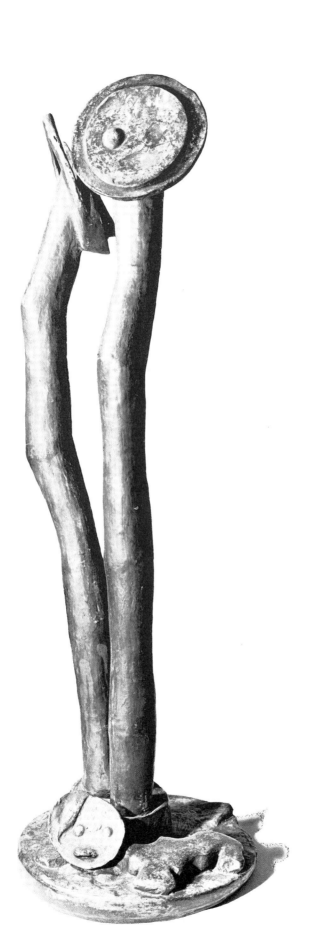

Chéri-Bibi, 1964-1975
Cast in bronze
Private collection

PUCE, FLEE, FLOH, 1967.   Collage on wood, 20″ × 17″ (51 × 43 cm)
Former collection of Alexander Iolas

Iolas at the beginning of 1968 under the title *Nothing and Its Double*, were smaller, but showed an equal concern for extremely detailed composition, and possessed qualities identical with those of *The Impeccable, The Burial Vault of the Innocents, Puce Flee Floh*.

His painting is more frankly oriented toward a smiling tranquillity, but to be sure it does not disdain an occasional touch of provocation and a conspiratorial wink (*The Garden of France, For a School of Monsters*), even changing into brilliant raillery in *Parthenogenesis of a Constellation*, which occupied the place of honor at the Salon of May 1968. Each day, however, it is increasingly obedient to his constant need to exalt his sense of the universal and the cosmic, as was already demonstrated in his exhibition of 1964, with *Here Are Three Earthquakes* and *The Moon Is a Silent Nightingale*. The repetition of early themes now transformed, in *The Last Forest* and *The Air Washed with Water*, ratifies the felicitous harmony which he has achieved after all his patient and persistent activity, that profound harmony between the imaginary and the lived, the visible and the invisible, that broadening to infinity of a world open to confidence and happiness, as he has always secretly dreamed of it.

Conclusion

A prince of the spirit, equally
capable of conquering and controlling matter.

What, in brief, can we learn from this life so full of a variety of incidents, and from Ernst's work, the exceptional scope and steadfast unity of which has become evident in recent inventories?

The omnipresence of the man, that is, of the creator, is extremely evident, even when he claims to conceal it under the benevolent effects of chance. His ecstatic but lucid gaze upon the world is always directed toward that broad area which is located beyond the real and which he perceives intensely and spontaneously. He belongs to the royal line of visionaries, with Novalis and Arnim, and is able to divine every sign concealed by external appearances. However, like the Primitives, and like his beloved Caspar David Friedrich, he is revolted by unnecessaryy vehemence and false pathos; he prefers calm, the unforeseen (in which he brings about the welling up of uneasy expectation), and tension. There is in his work a certain discrete, underlying anguish of living, anguish in the face of fate and the cruelty of destiny. Fantastic animals, masked phantoms, and grimacing demons who have surged up out of the night of time appear only episodically. The constantly hovering menace emanates from the surrounding nature, which, prophetically, disintegrates and decomposes under his brush, and for many years is heavy with a violently hostile tension.

The poet dominates in Ernst himself, and throughout his work, through the flood of images which he invents with tireless prodigality, and the verbal wealth he uses as an auxiliary and, more frequently, as an indispensable complement.

To what extent can he be accused of taking his principal sources from the works of Freud? The question has often been discussed. To be sure, very early in his career (before the First World War) he had learned from his friend Karl Otten of the Viennese master's doctrines, and at that time he applied them in his initial specialization. The very atmosphere of Cologne predisposed him to attach great importance to the dream, as to all prophetic signs. Undoubtedly he agrees with the theory regarding the role played by childhood events, which he readily subjects to a genuine clinical examination. In addition, he feels that while the dream is always the fulfillment of a wish, it also becomes the «substitute for a childhood scene modified by transferral into a recent phase.» He also emerges from it in order to «avoid the development of anguish and other types of distressing effects,» and to benefit from «the tremendous work of condensation of the thoughts in the dream,» in accordance with the same interpretation given by Freud. However, he concedes the importance of the activity performed during waking hours, and is closer to the position upheld by F. Paulhan in 1889: «I have often thought that there could be a certain deformation or rather re-formation of the dream when it is remembered ... the systematizing tendency of the imagination could very well complete after the subject's awakening what it began during sleep. Thus the actual rapidity of thought would be seemingly increased by the improvements made by the awakened imagination.»

The truth is that Ernst is too jealous of his independence to give his allegiance to a theory, submit to principles, or yield to any fixed position which is likely to interfere with his need for expression and his desire for constant renewal. He has always preferred to retain a wide margin of liberty, to explore the intermediate areas and the blurred borderlines between the subconscious and the preconscious, in order to retain a certain control. Is not the freedom to devote himself to the dual work of combination and contrasting of images, which leads him to so many unusual comparisons, the essential factor in his activity, as he has so often said? Has he not laid the new bases for his private universe in the name of this unexpected dialectic?

Unlike most of his comrades he has no need to turn to artifice, organized excitement, or exhibitionism, and not one of his works is without a basis. Something wells up in him, from the depths of his being, for he is attentive to every intuition, premonition, warning, and promise of the future which he interprets in the world around him, in the sky, in all of nature. Every image is a meeting with an emotive memory; he scrutinizes it, describes it, arranges it with a haughty severity. He endows it with an astonishing power of seduction which arouses curiosity and finally fascinates the mind, so striking and almost obsessive is this image, both by its disconcerting visibility and the unwavering strangeness of its character. Through this intrinsic quality of his creation he is, as Carlo Sala has stressed, the successor of and heir to the heritage of Symbolism and the exploration of the interior world carried on by Gustave Moreau and Odilon Redon.

Our era is liberating itself from encroaching mechanization and showing an increasing desire for the miraculous. Alain Gheerbrant's excellent film «The Other Side of the Moon,» based to a great extent on canvases by Max Ernst, gave evidence of the artist's extraordinary ability to painlessly achieve the most complete dislocation. This permits the spectator to immediately enter a new and coherent universe which is always seductive thanks to the variegated spaces it offers. Moreover, this universe continually wears a smile which reexamines, with pretended innocence, its very foundations and its sempiternal justifications.

After the war Ernst, a Surrealist before the word existed, was the first to combine the resources of oneirism with a skillfully performed operation of demystification of all habits, conventions, and taboos. For him the irony which he uses with even greater ease and percussive force than Arp and Man Ray, his closest comrades in this regard, is as much the expression of a vigorous reaction against the lies of society as it is a means of personal defense. At the same time it is a crafty approach, since it is an invitation to the spectator to force him to think, to become aware, to examine himself. Every one of Ernst's works is at once a window on the imaginary, a summons, and an overture to a dialogue.

In that symbol of the bird which he very soon chose to personify himself, we find the sign, according to the Freudian interpretation, of a strong sensuality which was more active throughout his life than is thought, and in particular the characteristic of constant rebellion, the publicly proclaimed determination of a spirit that considers itself almost libertarian and consistently refuses to accept or respect the criteria, classifications, and

THE LAST FOREST, 1960-1969. Oil on canvas, 45″ × 51½″ (114 × 146 cm)
Former collection of the artist

customary norms of contemporary society. If he wishes to remain in this way above law and custom, undoubtedly it is in order to have greater possibilities of mocking — with what remarkable finesse! — the outmoded, anachronistic appearance, persistently echoed in all of his collages, of those laws and customs.

He places at the service of this continual revolt and examination of the merits of our mechanistic civilization his keen sense of sculptural requirements and a sagacious experience with the techniques and materials which fill us with wonder, and which make self-renewal possible for him at every moment of his life, in terms of the fertility of his own genius.

In all his inventions quickly adopted by other artists — collages, *assemblages, frottages,* and so on — he can easily be distinguished by his fundamental elegance, his refined sense of layout and careful composition, and his desire for maximum economy of means. With extreme ease he experiments with every genre, adopts every method — engraving, for example, and even sculpture, in which he makes innovations uninhibitedly and without problems. His virtuosity, in the best sense of the term, blossoms particularly in his painting. Here, unlike so many other Surrealists, he is in complete possession of his craft, and displays a very confident judgment in the application of the scale of tonal values and the orchestration of colors. Did he not demonstrate his attainments and skill during his years of apprenticeship in Cologne, years which must not be overlooked?

Spanning the centuries, he is a successor to the old Rhenish masters, to whom he pledged a faithful veneration, by his lofty style, exquisite urbanity, vigilant sensitivity, and constant return to the world of nature around him, his childhood memories of which (especially his forest memories) are forever vivid.

With a consummate skill unequaled among his contemporaries, he is able to turn to best account the least important elements — wood, wallpaper, fabrics, etc. — in order to intimately associate them with his language and endow them with an astonishing power of expression. Here again his activity is of prize importance in this area, in which, like Picabia, but in a more vigilant, more carefully thought out and coherent manner, he has never ceased to explore every possible combination and to play an unquestionably genuine pioneering role, from beginning to end of his career.

Fully conscious of his responsibilities as an artist and a creator, Max Ernst has been able to assume them with smiling sovereignty, a tranquil courage despite the dangers confronted and the very distressing tribulations he was obliged to face, and an exemplary lucidity, all in addition to his now universally recognized merits.

His fruitful labor, patient persistence, prodigious intelligence, and the scope of the outstanding work he has produced in most phases of art, incontestably give him a place of leadership among those artists of our age who are not only visionaries but are also sincerely devoted to the human condition.

BIOGRAPHY

1891 Max Ernst born on April 2 in Brühl (near Cologne), where his father is a teacher of deaf-mutes.

1896 First drawings.

1897-1908 Attends grammar and high schools in Brühl. Enthusiast of Max Stirner, Flaubert, the occult. After final examination, leaves high school for the University of Bonn.

1908 Begins to study philosophy; also studies art history with Worringer. Learns about psychiatry; makes frequent visits to the insane asylum.

1909 Devotes himself entirely to painting; is influenced by Van Gogh, Gauguin, Monet, and later Macke (whose friend he becomes), Kandinsky, Delaunay.

Joins in the activities of "Das Junge Rheinland," where he meets Johannes T. Kühlemann, Karl Otten, and several painters.

1912 Visits the Sonderbund and the Futurist Exhibition in Cologne.

Exhibits several works at Friedrich Cohen's bookshop in Bonn and the Galerie Feldmann in Cologne.

1913 Meets Apollinaire and Delaunay at Macke's home. Collaborates in the First Autumn Salon organized by "Der Sturm" in Berlin.

1914-1918 Visits Paris early in 1914 and makes acquaintance of Arp, who becomes his most faithful friend. In the war for the duration, but tries to escape its destructive hold and takes refuge in his art. In January 1916 Der Sturm organizes an exhibition of his works and those of Georg Muche. His works are also exhibited in Zurich in April 1917 at the second exhibition of the Galerie Dada. Returns to Cologne in 1918. Marries Luise Straus.

1919 Becomes acquainted with Baargeld; with him (and later Arp), founds the Dada Central Office W/3, which attracts Freundlich, Hoerle, and others. British occupation authorities confiscate catalogues and posters of the first exhibition of the group. Publishes *Fiat Modes*, which also arouses vigorous reactions.

1920-1921 Birth of his son, Jimmy (1920). Second and last Dada Exhibition in Cologne, with Arp, Baargeld, Ernst, Picabia, and Tzara; it is closed by the police, and the catalogues and posters are confiscated. First exchange of letters with Breton, who invites Ernst to exhibit his collages in Paris. *La Mise sous Whisky Marin* takes place in May 1921 at the bookshop *Au Sans Pareil*. Major display of Dada art on the eve of the exposition. Vocations in the Tyrol with Arp, Tzara, and their women companions; joined by Breton and his new wife. The crisis in the Dada movement begins. Paul and Gala Eluard visit him in Cologne; they immediately become friends.

1922 After a troubled summer in the Tyrol with Eluard, Tzara, Arp and Josephson, Ernst settles in Paris, where *Les Malheurs des Immortels* has just been published. Is present at the experiments with automatic writing with Breton, Crevel, Desnos, Ribémont-Dessaignes. Sees a great deal of Man Ray and Picabia. Paints *Le Rendez-vous des Amis*.

1923 Despite difficult conditions, produces major works.

1924 Travels in Indochina with the Eluards. Upon his return, enthusiastically welcomes the publication of the Surrealist Manifesto.

1925 Discovers in the *frottage* method, a way of "forcing inspiration."

1926 Publication of *Histoire Naturelle*. Collaborates with Miró for the ballet "Romeo and Juliet." Exhibition at the Galerie Van Leer-Mouradian.

1927 Marries Marie-Berthe Aurenche.

1928 Exhibition at the Galerie Georges Bernheim.

1929 Publication of the collage-novel *La Femme 100 têtes*. Forms friendship with Alberto Giacometti. Participates in the film "L'âge d'or," with Bunuel and Dali.

1931 First exhibition in New York at the Julien Lévy Gallery.

1933 Ernst's name is placed on the Nazi regime's list of proscribed persons.

1934 Publishes another collage-novel, *Une Semaine de Bonté*. Visits Switzerland with Giacometti.

1936 Participates in the Museum of Modern Art exhibition in New York. Leaves Marie-Berthe Aurenche.

1937 Friendship with Leonora Carrington, with whom he settles in Saint-Martin-d'Ardèche.

1938 Sets for "Ubu enchaîné." Breaks with the Surrealist out of friendship toward Eluard.

1939-1940 Is interned several times as enemy alien; is released or escapes. Decides to take refuge in the United States, which he reaches via Spain.

1941 Resides in New York and in California. Marries Peggy Guggenheim. Is cordially welcomed by young painters.

1942 Despite special issue of *View* devoted to him, his exhibitions in New York, Chicago, and New Orleans are "complete flops."

1943 Meets Dorothea Tanning. Spends summer in Arizona.

1944 On Long Island, produces several sculptures.

1945 Exhibition at the Galerie Denise René in Paris.

1946-1947 Marries Dorothea. Settles in Sedona, Arizona, where he builds a house and creates wall sculptures.

1948 Unsuccessful exhibition at the Knoedler Gallery.

1948 Another unsuccessful exhibition in Beverly Hills, California.

1949 Trip to Europe.

1950 Major exhibition at the Galerie René Drouin in Paris.

1951 Retrospective in Brühl.

1952 Retrospective in Houston. Lectures in Hawaii.

1953 Returns to Paris, and takes a studio in the Impasse Ronsin. Successful exhibitions in Knokke Het Zoute and Cologne.

1954 Wins First Prize at the Venice Biennial. Shortly thereafter settles at Huismes in Touraine.

1956 Retrospective in Berne.

1957 Exhibits in New York.

1958 Becomes a French citizen.

1959 Presents a retrospective in Paris at the Musée National d'Art Moderne. Is awarded the Grand Prix National des Arts.

1961 Retrospective at the Museum of Modern Art in New York, and at the Gallery "Le Point Cardinal" in Paris.

1962 Retrospectives in London and Cologne.

1963 Retrospective in Zurich.

1965 Exhibitions in Paris (Galerie Iolas) and Geneva.

1966 Exhibitions in New York (Jewish Museum), Venice, and Vence.

1967 Exhibitions of graphic work in Hamburg, Worpswede, and Prague. Exhibition at "Le Point Cardinal" in Paris.

1968 Settles at Seillans (Var). Exhibits in Vence and Barcelona.

1969 Retrospective in Stockholm and Amsterdam. Exhibition in Turin.

1970 Retrospective in Stuttgart.

1970-1972 The Menil Collection travels to Hamburg, Hannover, Frankfurt, Berlin, Cologne, Paris, Marseille, Grenoble, Strasbourg, and Nantes.

1976 Max Ernst dies in Paris.

BIBLIOGRAPHY

CATALOGUES RAISONNÉS

SPIES, Werner. *Collagen Inventar und Widerspruch.* Cologne: De Menil Foundation and DuMont Schauberg, 1974.

LEPPIEN, Helmut and SPIES, Werner. *Das graphische Werk.* Cologne: De Menil Foundation and DuMont Schauberg, 1975.

MEKTEN, Sigrid and Günter, SPIES, Werner. *OEuvre Katalog 1906-1925.* Cologne: De Menil Foundation and DuMont Schauberg, 1975.

MEKTEN, Sigrid and Günter, SPIES, Werner. *OEuvre Katalog 1925-1929.* Cologne: De Menil Foundation and DuMont Schauberg, 1976.

MEKTEN, Sigrid and Günter, SPIES, Werner. *OEuvre Katalog 1929-1938.* Cologne: De Menil Foundation and DuMont Schauberg, 1979.

MEKTEN, Sigrid and Günter, SPIES, Werner. *OEuvre Katalog 1939-1953.* Cologne: De Menil Foundation and DuMont Schauberg, 1987.

WRITINGS BY MAX ERNST

"Vom Werden der Farbe" in *Der Sturm*, 5, Berlin, August 1917.

"Inspiration to Order" in *This Quarter* 5 (September 1932), 1, pp. 79-85.

"Au-delà de la peinture" in *Cahiers d'Art* 6-7, 1937.

Écritures. (Writings 1919-1970, ed. by René Bertelé). Paris: Gallimard, 1971.

WORKS ON MAX ERNST AND HIS TIME

ALEXANDRIAN, Sarane. *Max Ernst.* Paris: Filipacchi, 1971.

BAATSCH, Henri-Alexis, BAILLY, Jean-Christophe, and JOUFFROY, Alain. *Max Ernst, apprentissage, énigme, apologies.* Paris: Bourgeois, 1976.

BARR, Alfred H. *Fantastic Art, Dada, Surrealism.* New York: Museum of Modern Art, 1947.

BLAVIER, Beatrix. *Max Ernst: Murals for the home of Paul and Gala Eluard, Eaubonne, 1923.* M.A. thesis, Rice University, Houston, Texas, 1986. Ann Arbor, Michigan: UMI, 1986.

BOUSQUET, Joë and TAPIE, Michel. *Max Ernst.* Paris: Drouin, 1950.

BRETON, André. *Le Surréalisme et la peinture.* New York: Brentano, 1945.

CHADWICK, Whitney. *Myth in Surrealist Painting, 1929-1939.* Doctoral dissertation, Pennsylvania State University. Ann Arbor, Michigan: UMI, 1980.

ERNST, Jimmy. *Nicht gerade ein Stilleben. Erinnerungen an meinen Vater Max Ernst.* Cologne: Kippenheuer and Witsch, 1985.

ESTIENNE, Charles. *Le Surréalisme.* Paris: Gründ, 1956.

FISCHER, Lothar. *Max Ernst in Selbstzeugnissen und Bilddokumenten.* Reinbeck: Rowohlt, 1969.

GAFFE, René. *Peintures à travers Dada et le Surréalisme.* Brussels: Éditions des Artistes, 1952.

GATT, Giuseppe. *Max Ernst.* Lucerne: Kunstkreis, 1969.

GIMFERRER, Père. *Max Ernst ou la dissolution de l'identité.* Paris: Société du Livre, 1979.

GUGGENHEIM, Peggy. *Surrealism.* London: Faber, 1936.

GUGGENHEIM, Peggy. *My Life with Max Ernst.* New York: Dial, 1946.

JANCO, Marcel and BOLLIGER, Hans. *Dada (1916-1922).* Teufen: Niggli, 1957.

JEAN, Marcel. *Histoire de la peinture surréaliste.* Paris: Seuil, 1959.

KONNERTZ, Winfried. *Max Ernst, Zeichnungen, Aquarelle, bermalungen, Frottagen.* Cologne, 1980.

LAKE, Johannes auf der. *Skulpturen von Max Ernst: aesthetische Theorie und Praxis.* Doctoral dissertation, Ruhr-Universität, Bochum, 1985. Frankfurt, New York: Lang, 1986.

LARKIN, David, ed. *Max Ernst.* New York: Ballantine, 1975.

LEFFIN, Gudrun. *Bildtitel und Bildlegenden bei Max Ernst: ein interdisziplinärer Beitrag zur Kunst des zwanzigsten Jahrhunderts.* Doctoral dissertation, University of Cologne, 1987. Frankfurt, New York: Lang, 1988.

LEGGE, Elizabeth M. *Max Ernst, the psychoanalytic sources.* Doctoral dissertation, Ann Arbor, Michigan: UMI, 1989.

LEPPIEN, Helmut R. *Max Ernst FP2: Der große Wald.* Stuttgart, 1967.

LIPPARD, Lucy R. *The technical innovations of Max Ernst.* Unpublished M.A. thesis, Institute of Fine Arts, New York University, 1962.

LEVY, Julien. *Surrealism.* New York: Black Sun, 1936.

MOTHERWELL, Robert, ed. *Max Ernst, Beyond Painting.* New York: Wittenborn and Schulz, 1948.

PATYK, U. *Max Ernst und Paul Delvaux. Bildstruktur und Erzählmodi in den Bildern zwischen 1938 und 1960.* Frankfurt, New York: Lang, 1988.

PENROSE, Roland. *Max Ernst's Celebes.* Newcastle upon Tyne, 1972.

PRETZELL, Lothar and Loni, ed. *Max Ernst: Gemälde und Graphik 1920-1950.* Stuttgart, 1952.

QUINN, Edward, ed. *Max Ernst.* Boston: New York Graphic Society, 1977.

RUBIN, William S. *Dada and Surrealist Art.* New York, 1969.

RUSSELL, John. *Max Ernst. Life and Work.* New York: Abrams, 1967.

SALA, Carlo. *Max Ernst et la démarche onirique.* Paris: Klincksieck, 1970.

SANOUILLET, Michel. *Dada à Paris.* Paris, 1965.

SCHAMONI, Peter. *Max Ernst. "Maximiliana, The Illegal Practice of Astronomy. Hommage à Dorothea Tanning".* Boston: New York Graphic Society, 1974.

SCHNEEDE, Uwe. *Max Ernst.* New York, 1973.

SPIES, Werner. *Max Ernst.* New York: Abrams, 1969.

SPIES, Werner. *Max Ernst 1950-1970. Die Rückkehr der schönen Gärtnerin.* Cologne: DuMont Schauberg, 1971. *Max Ernst: The Return of La Belle Jardinière.* New York, 1972.

SPIES, Werner. *Max Ernst Loplop: The artist's other self.* London: Thames and Hudson, 1983.

SPIES, Werner. *Max Ernst, Frottagen.* Stuttgart: Hatje, 1986.

TANNING, Dorothea. *Birthday.* Santa Monica: Lapis Press, 1986.

TRIER, Eduard. *Max Ernst.* Recklinghausen: Bongers, 1959.

WALDBERG, Patrick. *Max Ernst.* Paris: Pauvert, 1958.

WALDBERG, Patrick. *Le Surréalisme.* Geneva: Skira, 1962.

WALDBERG, Patrick. *Chemins du Surréalisme.* Brussels, 1965.

WALDBERG, Patrick. *Max Ernst, peintures pour Eluard.* Paris, 1969.

SELECTED BOOKS ILLUSTRATED BY MAX ERNST

KUHLEMAN, Johannes Th. *Dichtungen.* Cologne-Ehrenfeld: Kairos, 1919.

Fiat Modes. Cologne: Schlömich, 1919.

Les Malheurs des Immortels, revealed by Paul Eluard and Max Ernst. Paris: Librairie Six, 1922. *Misfortunes of the Immortals.* New York, 1943.

ELUARD, Paul. *Répétitions.* Paris: Au Sans Pareil, 1922.

ELUARD, Paul. *Au Défaut du silence.* Paris, 1926.

La Femme 100 Têtes. Introduction by André Breton. Paris: Carrefour, 1929. Reprint, Paris, 1956.

Rêve d'une petite fille qui voulut entrer au Carmel. Paris: Carrefour, 1930. *A Little Girl Dreams of Taking the Veil.* New York: Braziller, 1982.

ARP, Hans. *Gedichte: Weisst du Schwarzt du.* Zurich: Pra, 1930.

CREVEL, René. *Mr. Knife and Miss Fork.* Paris: The Black Sun Press, 1931.

Une Semaine de Bonté ou Les Sept Éléments Capitaux. Paris: Jeanne Bucher, 1934.

BRZEKOWSKI, Jan. *Zacisniete dookota ust.* New York: Wittenborn and Schultz, 1934.

BRETON, André. *Le Château étoilé.* Paris, 1936.

PERET, Benjamin. *Je sublime.* Paris: Éditions surréalistes, 1936.

CARRINGTON, Leonora. *La Maison de la peur.* Paris: Parisot, 1938.

CARRINGTON, Leonora. *La Dame ovale.* Paris: G.L.M., 1939.

ELUARD, Paul. *Chanson complète.* Paris: Gallimard, 1939.

ELUARD, Paul and ERNST, Max. *À l'intérieur de la vue.* Paris: Seghers, 1947.

At the eye level. Bevely Hills, Californie: The Copley Galleries, 1949.

PERET, Benjamin and ERNST, Max. *La Brebis galante.* Paris: Les Éditions premières, 1949.

CARROLL, Lewis. *La Chasse au Snark.* Paris: Les Éditions premières, 1950.

Das Schnabelpaar. Basel: Beyeler, 1953.

ARTAUD, Antonin. *Galapagos.* Paris: Broder, 1955.

Paramythen. Cologne: Galerie Der Spiegel, 1955.

HÖLDERLIN. *Poèmes.* Paris: Jean Hugues, 1961.

LECLERCQ, Léna. *La Rose est nue.* Paris: Jean Hugues, 1961.

Les Chiens ont soif. With a text by Jacques Prévert. Paris: Au Pont des Arts, 1964.

Maximiliana ou L'Exercice illégal de l'astronomie. Paris: Le Degré Quarante-et-un, 1964.

PARISOT, Henri. *Anthologie poétique.* Paris: Belfond, 1969.

RIBÉMONT-DESSAIGNES, G. *La Ballade du soldat.* Vence: Pierre Chave, 1972.

EXHIBITIONS

1961 *Max Ernst*. Museum of Modern Art, New York; Art Institute, Chicago. Catalog by William S. Lieberman, ed.

1962-1963 *Max Ernst*. Wallraf-Richartz Museum, Cologne; Kunsthaus, Zurich. Text by G. von der Osten and C. Giedion-Welcker; Catalog by H. Leppien.

1964-1965 *Max Ernst. Zwei-und-zwanzig Mikroben*. Galerie der Spiegel, Cologne. Texts by Hans Arp and A. Fabri.

1965 *Le Monde frotté à la mine de plomb par Max Ernst. Frottages de 1925-1965*. Galerie Benador, Geneva. Text by Max Ernst.
Max Ernst. Le Musée de l'Homme. La Pêche au soleil levant. Galerie Iolas, Paris. Text by Max Ernst.

1966 *Max Ernst. Peintures, collages récents*. Galerie Chave, Vence.
Max Ernst. Sculpture and recent paintings. The Jewish Museum, New York. Texts by Max Ernst, L.R. Lippard, A.P. de Mandiargues and J. Russell.

1967 *Max Ernst. Graphik 1919-1967*. Kunsthalle, Worpsede. Text by Jean Cassou.

1969 *Max Ernst malninger, collage, frottage, technigar, grafik, böckner, sculpturer 1917-1969*. Moderna Museet, Stockholm. With poems by Max Ernst.

1970 *Max Ernst*. Stedelijk Museum Amsterdam. Texts by Max Ernst and De Wilde, poems by P. Eluard, Lucebert, and J. Prévert.
Max Ernst. Gemälde, Plastiken, Collagen. Württembergischer Kunstverein, Stuttgart. Introduction by U.M. Schneede. Texts by W. Spies, H.R. Leppien, Max Ernst et al.
Max Ernst. OEuvre gravé, dessins, frottages et collages. Musée d'Art et d'Histoire, Geneva. Text by C. Goerg and E. Rossier.

1970-1971 *Das innere Gesicht. Die Sammlung De Menil*. Kunsthalle, Hamburg; Kestner-Gesellschaft, Hanovre; Kunstverein, Frankfurt; Akademie der Künste, Berlin, Kunsthalle, Cologne. *À l'intérieur de la vue*. Musée de l'Orangerie, Paris; Musée Cantini, Marseilles; Maison de la Culture, Grenoble; Ancienne Douane, Strasburg; Musée des Beaux-Arts, Nantes. Texts by W. Hofmann, W. Schmied and W. Spies.

1971 *Max Ernst. Lieux communs, décervelages*. Galerie A. Iolas, Paris.

1972 *Max Ernst. Jenseits der Malerei. Das graphische OEuvre*. Kestner Museum, Hanovre. Texts by E. Kästner and W. Spies.
Max Ernst. La Ballade du Soldat. Galerie Berggruen, Paris.

1972-1973 *Max Ernst ne peint plus! Peintures récentes*. Galerie Chave, Vence.

1973-1974 *Max Ernst. Inside the Sight. Paintings from the Menil Family Collection*. Institute for the Arts, Rice University, Houston, Texas; Nelson-Atkins Museum,

Kansas City, Missouri; The Art Institute, Chicago; Fogg Art Museum, Cambridge, Massachusetts. Texts by W. Hofmann, W. Schmied and W. Spies.

1975 *Max Ernst. A Retrospective*. The Solomon R. Guggenheim Museum, New York. Texts by T. Messer and D. Waldeman.
Max Ernst. Estampes et livres illustrés. Bibliothèque nationale, Paris. Text by Étienne Dennery.
Max Ernst. Galeries nationales du Grand Palais, Paris. Texts by P. Hulten, W. Spies and G. Viatte.

1975-1976 *Max Ernst. Prints, Collages and Drawings 1919-1972*. Scottish Art Council, Edinburgh.

1978 *10 x Max Ernst*. Kunstsammlung Nordrhein-Westfalen, Düsseldorf.

1980 *Max Ernst in Köln. Die rheinische Kunstszene bis 1922*. Wallraf-Richartz Museum, Cologne. Catalog by W. Herzogenrath, ed. Texts by D. Hackes, U. Bohnen and K. Dieckhöfer.

1981 *Max Ernst: Gemälde, Skulpturen, Collagen, Frottagen, Zeichnungen, Druckgraphik und Bücher. Verzeichnis der Bestände*. Kunstmuseum, Hanovre with the Sprengel Collection. Texts by B. Holaczek and J. Büchner.

1982 *Max Ernst's Histoire naturelle: Leaves Never Grow on Trees*. Arts Council of Great Britain, London.

1983 *Max Ernst*. Fondation Maeght, Saint-Paul-de-Vence. Catalog by J.-L. Prat. Text by W. Spies.

1984 *Max Ernst. Fragments of Capricorn and other sculptures*. Herstand, Arnold and Co., New York. Text by Werner Spies.

1984-1985 *Max Ernst. "La Femme 100 têtes."* Max Ernst Kabinett, Brühl. Catalog by Jürgen Pech.

1985 *Max Ernst. Landschaften*. Galerie Beyeler, Basel.

1986 *Max Ernst. "Das Karmelitenmädchen."* Max Ernst Kabinett, Brühl. Catalog by Jürgen Pech.
Max Ernst. Beyond Surrealism. A Retrospective of the artist's books and prints. New York Public Library, New York; Museum of Art, University of Michigan, Ann Arbor. Texts by A. Hyde-Greet, E.M. Maurer, R. Rainwater.

1986 *Max Ernst*. Fundación Juan March, Madrid. Texts by Werner Spies.

1987 *Histoires de forêt: Max Ernst*. Musée des Beaux-Arts, Nantes. Texts by H.-C. Cousseau, W. Spies, J.C. Bailly, Max Ernst, V. Rousseau, and D. Ottinger.

1988-1989 *Max Ernst. Die Welt der Collage*. Kunsthalle, Tübingen; Kunstmuseum, Bern; Kunstmuseum Nordrhein-Westfalen, Düsseldorf. Text by Werner Spies.

1989 *Max Ernst. Illustrierte Bücher und druckgraphische Werke*. Kunstmuseum, Bonn. Texts by K. Schmidt et al.

ILLUSTRATIONS

"À travers les âges" 77

After Us-Motherhood 41

Anger of the Red Man (The) 12

Anthropomorphic Figure 39

Appeasement 58

Birds (The) 71

Birth of a Galaxy 78

Blessed Virgin Chastises the Infant Jesus (The) 29

Bottle (The) 70

"Caveau des Innocents (Le)" 76

Chéri-Bibi 83

Collage from "Une Semaine de Bonté" 51

Conjugal Diamonds (The) 6

Cry of the Gull (The) 64

Dadaville 19

Earth with a Lie on ist Lips (The) 68

Entire City (The) 43

Escaper (The) 23

Euclid 54

Europe after the Rain 46-47

Eve the Only One Left 20, 21

Fête at Seillans (The) 73

Foresta Imbalsamata (La) 42

Garden Airplane Trap 48

Gramineous bicycle... (The) 9

"Grand Albert (Le)" 56

Hat in the Hand, Hat on the Head 10

"Heure Bleue (L')" 55

Horde (The) 40

Hunter (The) 30

Illustration from "Une Semaine de Bonté" ... 34

Interior of Sight: the Egg (The) 37

Katharina Ondulata 15

Landscape with Germ of Wheat 44

Last Forest (The) 87

Leaves, Birds and Grapes 31

33 Little Girls Set out to Hunt the White Butterflies 65

Marriage of Heaven and Earth (The) 61

Monument to the Birds 66

October 80

Oedipus Rex 11

Origin of the Pendulum (The) 7

Painting for Young People 63

Person in Anger 24

Picture Poem 17

"Portrait d'ancêtre" 74

Puce, Flee, Floh 84

"Saint Sulpice" 75

Sea-Shells 5

Sea, Sun, Earthquake 53

"Sérénité" 67

She Keeps her Secret 14

She Refuses to Understand 38

Sunday Guests 27

Swaying Woman (The) 26

Tangled Lightning 79

Temptation of Saint Anthony (The) 45

Twin Souls 82

Vision Provoked by the Nocturnal Aspect of the Porte Saint Denis 32

When Sirens Awake Reason Goes to Sleep ... 62

Woman of Tours 59